THE BEST
MEN'S
STAGE MONOLOGUES

2022

THE BEST MEN'S STAGE MONOLOGUES 2022

Edited by **Debbie Lamedman**

S&K

Smith and Kraus Publishers

2022

A Smith and Kraus Book

177 Lyme Road
Hanover, NH 03755
Editorial: 603.643.6431
To Order: 1.877.668.8680

www.smithandkraus.com

The Best Men's Stage Monologues 2022 Copyright © 2022

Manufactured in the United States of America

ISBN 978-1-57525-967-3
ISSN 2164-2346

Cover design/interior formatting by Vickie Swisher, Studio 2020

For information about custom editions, special sales, education and corporate
purchases, please contact Smith and Kraus or 603.643.6431

TABLE OF CONTENTS

FOREWORD

Thirty-two years ago, Smith & Kraus began publishing anthologies of the best men's and women's stage monologues. Thirty-two years ago in 1990! Remember 1990?

Many playwrights have told me they "grew up" with these books. Used them almost like a Bible for classes and auditions. Never dreaming that one day, their writing would be included in one of these collections. And now, here we are. Thirty-two years later. 2022. Who could have ever predicted back then, where we, the theatre community, would find ourselves today?

The pandemic. Oy. What a huge toll it has taken in every capacity. And the arts? We've taken our hits with canceled performances, closings of theatres, and a shift from live performances to a virtual stage.

And yet, the writers in this book have never been more prolific. There is something about a monologue that adapts quite perfectly to a Zoom platform. You actually don't lose the intimacy of the moment at all. Perhaps you even gain some. The opportunities for monologue work seem to be expanding as venues in the virtual world continue to develop and open.

Here, in this book, you will find 70 very diverse monologues written for men. These pieces present great acting challenges, and actors will have the pleasure of sinking their teeth into this sublime material while continuing to perfect their craft in their online or in-person workshops.

These monologues all come from plays, and should you want to read the play in its entirety, I recommend you contact the playwright or their representative. The contact information can be found in the Rights & Permission section at the back of the book.

I also encourage you to discover more about the writers featured here. Many have their own websites which are included on their monologue page, but playwrights are now able to keep an online portfolio of their work in the largest digital library of scripts for living playwrights known as the New Play Exchange. https://newplayexchange.org/ If you are a writer, director, actor, dramaturg, or simply a lover of plays, I highly recommend checking out NPX.

As Hamlet famously said, "The purpose of playing, whose end, both at the first and now, was and is, to hold as 'twere the mirror up to nature: to show virtue her feature, scorn her own image, and the very age and body of the time his form and pressure." Now, in 2022, these monologues are representations of the life we are currently living. The sorrows, the challenges, the humanness of our lives are right here in these pages.

So, go. Read these pieces. Act these pieces. They will seem familiar to you as you hold the mirror up to nature and realize that art is indeed life.

~ **Debbie Lamedman**
February 2022
https://www.debbielamedman.com/

THE MONOLOGUES

N

David Alex

EDDY, 20s, a white male caregiver for MRS. PAGE, a passionate social and political elderly African American woman. EDDY is responding to her explanation of the contradictions of race and privilege.

EDDY

Nobody asks me what it's like to be white. Black people look at me wondering, how racist is he, did his ancestors own slaves, does he think he's better than me? You talk, talk, talk about being an individual. How you made something of yourself with all your gigabytes. That's great. Well, whatever I'm making of myself, I'm an individual too. I'm me, one person, not a legacy. Now tell me the truth — when I first walked through the door, did you see me, Eddy — or did you see a white person you think represents the legacy of bigotry and racism you've confronted? Because, when I first walked in the door, it didn't look to me like you saw Barry Goldwater …

You mock me when I say I don't see color and then mock me again by saying I should see your legacy. Did you see mine? … You claim the Constitution gave you the liberty to be an individual. As if the Constitution's what, color blind? It's not … How can a person, any person, have that liberty when they're treated as less than equal by some states. Not everyone takes off from the same starting line. You're the one who's blind; we really need the federal government.

Information on this playwright may be found at
https://newplayexchange.org/users/1638/david-alex

TALKING TO STRANGERS IN BARS

Glenn Alterman

MARV is in his thirties or forties. He has just met Maryanne in a bar during Happy Hour. They've had a couple of drinks. He's very attracted to her and finally asks her if they could go back to her place. She finds his request to go back to her place unpleasant. She's about to leave when he decides to level with her.

MARV

(Putting his drink down, looking at her for a moment) My name's Marv; Marvin. And I'm here in the city on business. I'm staying at an inexpensive hotel, midtown. My company's on a limited budget. It's actually kind of a dump, where I'm staying. So I was sitting in my crummy room feeling … a little lonely. So I decided to go out and have a drink. Saw this place, looked okay, came in. Happy Hour. And well, I saw you, *(smiling)* and got happy … Look, I really don't know you, don't even know your name. But I like you. And for me, right now, that's enough. I like talking to you, looking at you. And, well, I thought the idea of bringing you back to my cheap hotel room would be *disrespectful*. So what I'm saying … We don't have to go anywhere. We can just sit here and talk for as long as you like. Then whenever you want, you can leave, go. But for now would you just sit here … and talk with me? *(Smiling)* I promise, no more funny pick-up lines. Then when we're through talking, we'll just say good-bye. A happy, Happy Hour. Strangers. Friends. Talk-talk-talk. *(He lifts his glass, takes a sip, smiles at her. Softly)*. Okay, I'm through.

Information on this playwright may be found at www.glennaltermanplaywright.com

GLIDERS

Rita Anderson

CURTIS, age open. CURTIS is a working-class man with a low-paying job at a factory. He is married to Deborah, a waitress. It is 1969, during the Apollo moon landing mission, and CURTIS relays his hopes to his wife.

CURTIS

Your mom and your big sister, Geraldine, both act like they want everything to stay the same. As if *time* could or should stand still. And I just can't stand it, Deborah. The idea of things staying the same forever. And nothing ever changing. Just like with the astronauts. Here we sit on our couch, drinking warm beer and wondering how we're gonna make next month's rent. Meanwhile, those astronauts are out there, suspended somewhere in the unknown, just floating in that eternity of blackness overhead. I work in a gotdam factory, for Christsakes. And you? Your life is about scrubbing toilets and waiting tables. But those astronauts? They're out there pushing boundaries, not other people's *buttons*. And redefining everything we *thought* we knew. And risking it all. *(Pause.)* I wish I knew the stars. I mean, maybe I can find the Big Dipper. But. Imagine the courage, Deborah. For real. To board that rocket ship with no guarantee that they would even make it off the ground. Or that they'll ever get back to Earth. Or see their families again. And I am so proud of human beings for figuring it out. Like how to build such a ship that can pierce the stars themselves. And to build a better dream. They're dreaming new dreams like no one's ever dreamed before and *finding* ways to make them *happen*. Breaking records! Making history. I cannot even imagine what it feels like to be so, so *special* and to live such a large life. Why they must eat stardust for breakfast! It just. Makes me wish that things weren't so … That I wasn't so. Ordinary.

Information on this playwright may be found at https://rita-anderson.com

SHIMMER

David-Matthew Barnes

TITO BENAVIDES, early 20s, is the object of many desires and he knows it. Fed up with the sexual advances of the many married women he works for, TITO explains to his client Claudia Veramonte that there is much more than meets the lustful eye in the life an attractive pool boy.

TITO

Us pool boys have a bad reputation. It might surprise you to know most of us are doing this shitty work to pay our way through school. Call me whatever you want, Claudia, but this is not my goal in life. Serving as your eye candy fantasy boy is not how I enjoy spending my time. Cleaning pools is not exactly what I was born to do. Yes, you're right. I'm well aware of how attractive I am. I know lust when I see it and I see it a lot. Every day. Everywhere I go. People look at me with a longing, like something they want to desperately touch, but they know they never can or will. I'm out of reach. I'm something they've imagined or dreamed about. Do I use this to my advantage? Hell yeah, I do. I'm not an idiot. I know how much lonely people will pay just to watch me take my shirt off, walk around their backyard in a pair of shorts, and clean their pools they never swim in. I have to work out six times a week. I have to watch what I eat. I have to make sure I always smell good. The conversations are the tricky part. I make sure to mix in just enough innuendo to let them think there's a possibility, that I might suddenly decide to have sex with them right there and then. That's what they hope for. That's what they want. They don't care about knowing me. They don't want to follow me home and see what my life is like or hear my views on the state of the world or whether or not I've ever grieved over someone who died. They want me to keep my mouth shut, my shirt off, and my body perfect. That's all I am to them. That's all I am to you. A dumb pool boy with a hot body.

Information on this playwright may be found at
www.bluedasherpress.com

Edited by Debbie Lamedman   5

IT HAPPENED IN JEFFERSON SQUARE

Cris Eli Blak

TOMMY, Black, 30s, has decided to sue the police department after his best friend Monty, a police officer, witnesses the beating and murder of his own cousin at the hand of his fellow officers. This monologue, closing act one has TOMMY addressing the audience directly, scolding them for the truths they pretend to lead and the extent of the damage they do when their care is only based on convenience.

TOMMY

I have come to the most likely correct conclusion that no one cares. Not about you, not about me. Not about a goddamn one of us. Except for maybe your grandparents and, if you're lucky, one of your actual parents. Care is based upon convenience. No one cares about your ass until they feel obligated to or feel that it would be wrong if they did not. For example, a young girl is bullied for the entirety of her school career. She goes from kindergarten to freshman year of high school being pushed down stairs and assaulted in the bathroom. That is until she is diagnosed with leukemia. Then everyone loves her. Everyone states their support, has nothing but nice things to say about her. And if — or rather, in this situation — when she passes away, every brat who ever busted her head against a desk will act as if they were her best friends. They will speak on how they wish they knew her more than they did, how they wished she had more time. They will say that they care. And they will be lying. Everyone lies. And lies are easier than truth. See, if that young girl passed and those kids admitted to making her life a living hell, they would not appear to have a semblance of a heart. The truth is the truth but it is not light on the tongue.

Similarly, a young man is killed. For his entire life he has been nothing more or less than a nigger. He has been a nigger since birth. The doctor, aged sixty something, helped his mama birth him and internally the first thought he had was, "another nigger in the world, Lord help us." It is an uncomfortable thought but then, again, the truth usually is. So this young man grows up, seen as nothing but that label that was plastered on his forearm and then one day he is murdered and motherfuckers turn him into a martyr. They paint pictures of him, march for him, cry for him, pray for him — they would not have trusted him during his life. They would have avoided him, crossed the street at the sight of his Black ass, but in death it is better to seem clear of prejudice. It is better to seem that you care. Though you do not. Though you never have. You will pretend and act in the never-ending American showcase until you feel safe enough returning to your corner of the world where you are safe. Until a young man who looks quite a lot like the other young man is killed in very similar circumstances. Then you care again. Then you make a conscious effort to be heard and seen caring because if no one sees you caring then you are not important and your caring is pointless and why pretend that you're caring if no one can witness it? After all, it is more about you and it is more about image than it is about peace or love or simply giving a fuck about anyone who isn't the person looking back at you in the goddamn mirror.

So, yes, I feel that I am one hundred and ten percent correct in my observation that your caring is bullshit and that your care is cowardice and that your heart is nonexistent. It is barren, it is bare. It is naked. It is empty. You are empty. You are a liar. You are all liars. You are all searching desperately for relevance because you have none and will never have any unless you market yourself at the expense of a dead body. Fuck you and your care. Fuck you and your low-level performance art decorated to appear as activism. You don't care. And I don't care about you. The stark difference between the two of us is that I am not afraid to say so.

Information on this playwright may be found at
https://criseliblak.wixsite.com/my-site

MARTIN'S TREEHOUSE

Hilary Bluestein-Lyons

MARTIN, a 10-year-old boy, is explaining to their friend Dina why they can't talk to their mom about the lipstick they stole from her. The play calls for a non-binary actor in their 20s.

MARTIN

No, she doesn't want to talk about things with me. She never does. Don't you get it? Stop pushing me. You know, she hasn't even said one word to me about my dad dying. Not one word. Not since the funeral. I've never even been to a funeral before. I didn't know what to expect. And she got all mad at me when I was wearing sweatpants and a t-shirt. How was I supposed to know that I was supposed to wear a suit? So, I went and put on my suit, but the only tie I could find was a clip-on one from when I was like three years old or something. So, she had to go and get one of my dad's ties. It was a blue one, one my dad wore a lot. I noticed it had a small stain on it, but I didn't want to say anything to make her more mad. And of course, I didn't know how to tie the tie, so then she was mad that I didn't know how. And that my dad didn't show me. And that's when she said, "you're gonna have to step up now that your dad's gone." Step up? Step up to what? What does that even mean? Do more chores? Pay the bills? What? I'm only 10! I mean I guess I could've watched a YouTube video to learn how to tie a tie. But does that mean that I wasn't stepping up before? I mean my room's a mess, but it's not like she's in charge of cleaning it. What does she care, as long as I keep my door closed? And then, does it make it my fault? Is it my fault that my dad died? Because I didn't step up enough. I don't think a person could have heart failure because someone doesn't step up or clean their room or do enough. That doesn't cause someone's heart to fail, does it? I didn't even know that I had to wear a tie to a funeral, let alone a suit. Like how am I supposed to know unless someone tells me?

And no one tells me anything! Plus, the tie was way too long, so I looked stupid. I would've looked less stupid if I wore sweatpants and a t-shirt. It's not like anyone would've noticed me or cared, least of all my dad. And it was his funeral. He wouldn't've cared what I wore!

Information on this playwright may be found at
https://newplayexchange.org/users/12015/hilary-bluestein-lyons

TRACKS

John Patrick Bray

DAPPER DAN, 17, a Northern Dutchess county local who goes to a prep school, is hoping to woo JENNIE, 17, an aspiring songwriter who does not go to prep school. JENNIE has learned she is going to lose her favorite place by the tracks, where they are presently meeting, as a major train company is buying up all the land on the east side of the Hudson River for a proposed bullet train from NYC to Albany.

DAPPER DAN

And so, my Dad says that, um … with IBM basically gone, and like … NAFTA moving a bunch of other stuff to Central America, people have no reason to be here. And maybe if AmTrain comes along, they'll put in a station. Well. It's progress, right? *(Beat.)* I get why you, you know, don't want to lose this place. My dad says this used to be a make-out spot for townies. You know? So. Um. I suck at … what do you call them … words. Um. You wanna make out? *(Awkward beat. Clearly rejected.)* I love the spring fair, but I almost never go. We don't even get spring break until next week at Hawthorne Valley Waldorf, and even if we do, it's an hour trip each way. It kind of kills the potential for anything social happening. Unless you have a car. Which I do. I mean, I will. I'm just … I'll really pass the driver's test next time, you know? Um. How late do you think we'll be out? Just because I have school tomorrow. I just. I mean … I'm happy to be here with you. So. *(Beat.)* You know what you could do? About this place? You could do a letter writing campaign. You know? Get you and your friends to write letters to the governor. *(Beat. She's clearly unconvinced.)* It *could* work! They won't actually read them, but if there's enough of them, if you can get everyone around you to write a letter, and maybe, I don't know, inspire folks from other towns along the tracks, you might actually get a response just by the sheer, you know, volume of letters. What do you think? *(Beat. DAPPER DAN looks up as if hearing a train.)* Hear that train whistle? It's the sound of progress.

Information on this playwright may be found at www.johnpatrickbray.com

CANOPY

Rachael Carnes

*DANA, mature — late 50s through 80s — was expecting an
important callback from the doctor on Friday but missed it.
It's the weekend now, and DANA can't call back.*

DANA

I changed the batteries in the smoke alarm. Honey? Can you hear
me? They started beeping so I changed them ahead of schedule.
Should I write that down? Where do we write that kind of thing
down? Is it on the fridge? Or on this calendar? I want to do what
you want me to do — To do it right, you know? I want to be
helpful! They were chirping — This one was — It started chirping
and its light was flashing and that means its battery's dying so I
changed this one, but not the other ones so now this one is on
a different cycle than the others and I just want you to tell me
how you want me to record that? Where is it writ? Where is it
noted? Is it with the birthdays? Sweetie? Where is the birthday
calendar, for the kids and the grandkids and my sister? Where do
you keep that? Should I put this new smoke alarm information
with the birthday calendar? Can you hear me, honey? I just want
to follow your rules. I want to be successful. I can't do that if you
don't tell me what to do. Since you're not saying anything, I'm just
starting my own new calendar. I'm doing it. Right here on the
dog one. Right on this calendar! I'm getting a pen. Honey — I'm
flipping ahead six months! And I'm doing it — I'm writing 'smoke
alarm batteries' on this day in June. Huh — There's nothing else in
June. Honey, is this where we keep things? Is this calendar where
we keep appointments? There's nothing on here! This calendar is
from last year. Sweetie, why do we have a dog calendar from last
year? Well — I am still going to put 'smoke alarm batteries' on
June for this year — Even though it's last year. Because somebody
has to. You're not going. I'm the one who does stuff like that. I
remember the roof. We're on our fifth roof! Did you ever call them?

No. I did. And our taxes — I do our taxes. And I don't know when our grandchildren's birthdays are but I have a vague idea, so I'm putting them in last year's dog calendar, honey! The girl's in the spring sometime and the boy's in the fall. Done. Do you ever worry? That you might just go away? Like a smudge. I do. I worry all the time. I'm like a grease spot on a window, I haven't done anything. At least I don't feel like it? I went to an office. We went on some vacations — The kids grew up — I wrote checks for them. I cheered them on from the sidelines but there was always something I thought I'd become. Do you feel that way? Do you wish things were different? Do you have regrets? I mean — I'm not special. I don't really deserve to have 'regrets', it's not like I made choices that had consequences for anyone but myself. Maybe that's the point? If I'd lived bigger — I might be dead or in jail or famous for something or maybe all three! But I played it safe. I scheduled the roof maintenance. I paid our taxes. We paid off this house — The kids will get it. They'll probably sell. They'll take all our stuff to the thrift store. They told me that. Said there was nothing here they wanted. They like new things. New things don't last, but they look good. The kids say antlers are having a moment. They had a moment. So did beards. Beards are back. All the kids look like dwarves from the '40's. I feel like I missed out. You were here. You saw them grow up more than I did. I was in an office. I was in meetings. I was writing memos and — It's fine. Everything is fine. Honey — I don't know how to fill my day?

Information on this playwright may be found at
https://newplayexchange.org/users/16553/rachael-carnes

EVERYDAY AVIATION

Rachael Carnes

COREY, a dad in his 30s or 40s, futzes with technology for a minute, then stares into his laptop's video camera. It's Spring 2020, late at night. COREY looks away, then back again.

COREY

I thought I should do this. Leave this. I don't know. There's no blueprint. It seemed prudent?

There's a rhythm to the day and I love you and I get that we can roll out snacks and games but — So many headlines. So many stories. And we're just getting started. You don't know that — You're just a baby. Wide-eyed and content enough to have your mom and me home all the time. You crush me at UNO, kiddo! Undefeated Champion of the World! And I like reading to you. I'm worried: That cough you had on your last day of school (When was that?) hasn't gone away. All day, I beg you to blow your nose and then wash your hands. Tucking you in — You asked: When can you see your friends? We had that video conference? Remember? That was fun.

We blew out the candles for Sophie — We had an Oreo and she had a cupcake and we all sang?

I can't make you stop crying yourself to sleep. Your mother tries to anchor you, but we don't — Little man, I spend less time in this space where I feel safe every day, y'know?

I want to fight! And I want to curl in a ball and I want to cry and laugh and fall apart.

But I read you stories. And we stack blocks and play Legos and I feel the walls closing in and — What if they close all the way? What if the trap door opens, and takes me out? What if —

Oh, honey. What if the hole opens, and takes you from me?

Information on this playwright may be found at
https://newplayexchange.org/users/16553/rachael-carnes

ME OR YOU

Chima Chikazunga

CHAD, Black-American male, 30-40s. CHAD , laying down.
Nurse enters and hands him a phone. She wipes his forehead.
A soft smile, as he takes a deep breath

CHAD

I'm glad you called. It's been a while … but this hurts … THIS … And I know Tommy … But you don't need to apologize. *(laughs)* I know what you mean. But Life isn't about living. It's about what you do before you … *(takes a deep breath)* Wait for it. *(Exhales)*

You've been on my mind bro. I'm glad you called. Oh yeah, of course. I'm just … *(coughs)* it's like when we were kids and we'd get into trouble and you'd say … we'd look at each other, "It's me or you bro. Who's going first?" Remember that shit? *(coughs harder)* Sorry about that, where was I … oh yeah, actually … to be honest there was a time where I thought I had a friend. See, when I was a kid I used to go to day camp in the suburbs and I had this friend. We had to be about 7 or so and we were riding our bikes over to his house that day after camp. My friend was half Asian but what did I care? We were just kids. We didn't know anything about race like that; all we knew was about friends.

And I suddenly forgot where I was going with this. *(stops)* Oh yeah … So we are riding our bikes over to his house after camp because he's got a hoop in his driveway and his parents weren't there, so we could play. I used to always beat him at camp so that day we decided to play at his court because "he never loses there." So whatever, I don't care, and we're riding and I begin to notice that the houses are getting nicer. Like they are changing, from what my neighborhood houses look like to his. But I guess that's the norm because we crossed the tracks and seem to be heading towards the water. So anyway, we come across this guy sitting on the stoop of this church drinking a can of beer, but we really don't pay him any mind. Suddenly we hear, "Hey get that nigger out of here!" And I stop and I'm like, "who?" So I say, "Hey Tommy, I think that guy called you a nickel. You know him? Nickel is half a dime right? He know you are half Chinese? I don't get it and Tommy says, " No, keep riding. He wasn't talking to me, he was talking to you. He said nigger, not nickel." Not sure I even let it register but next thing I know, a beer can exploded in between us and I stopped. *(pause)* Long story short, Tommy's dad wasn't too far and spotted us. He was a cop and Tommy was shaken up afterwards. Tommy's dad went back by the church and arrested the guy.

(Beat) I hadn't thought about that story until after we stopped talking recently and THAT was because you called me a NIGGER. Sure we were drunk and things were said but my mind is racing with images — Black images … You're my friend, my brother. and I'm struggling with a lot and not knowing how to feel as I process this … but we live in an age where a white person can literally get away with murder with no consequences. And I'm thinking about this, all in this split second … did he deserve it? Emmitt. Because all I can see is his face. The before and the after, BUT WHY? Even after she confessed that she "made her story up" 60 years later.

Nothing happened … NOT A DAMN THING. His life … gone. 60 years is a long time to apologize. But we breathe the same air … bleed the same color blood.

And the craziest thing is how every day of my life … one word triggers a memory that was so hateful from someone that didn't even know me, when I was riding my bike with you that day Tommy. You were there, right by my side. But we were different then. And I know why you called … I don't need your apology. I don't need your understanding. I'm not mad … I love you bro. Life isn't about living. Life is about what you do before you die. And I'm glad you called. Because I get to tell you that I love you. *(coughs)* And your phone call means the world me my friend … I just want you to take that deep breath tomorrow or the next day or whenever … *(exhale)* … I'm not afraid or anything, I just need to hear something new other than what's going on in my head … breathe with me, Tommy … Hey Tommy, you there? Ok good. It's ok. *(coughs)* Stay with me …

(They breathe together. It can continue for as long as it takes. Then silence as he takes his last breath and phone drops ...)

Information on this playwright may be found at https://newplayexchange.org/users/9921/chima-chikazunga

WHAT I THOUGHT I KNEW

Alice Eve Cohen

MICHAEL, a 34-year-old freelance musician and actor from New Orleans. He and his fiancé Alice are meeting with an abortion doctor in his New York City office. After months of misdiagnoses, she has just found out that she's six months pregnant and that the baby is likely to have serious medical problems. After he tells Alice her legal options for an abortion this late in the pregnancy, the doctor asks MICHAEL what he's feeling.

MICHAEL

Me? Oh, Jesus. I feel … a lot of different things. I've seen Alice in the throes of this terrible unhappiness and … I don't recognize her. It's making her go crazy. For the first time in my life — and I come from an extremely conservative, southern Christian family where the abortion issue is completely — I've had to genuinely think about abortion rights. For the first time, I understand the importance of a woman's right to choose. But the equally compelling personal truth for me is that there's a baby. Our baby. My baby. And I don't care if she has a penis or two penises or three heads or … I can't stand the thought of this baby being aborted. So, if Alice has an abortion, I won't go to Wichita with her. And I might not be here when she gets back. I'll have my own unbearable sorrow about losing this baby, about endorsing this decision. But I don't want Alice to kill herself. So she should do what she needs to do.

Information on this playwright may be found at
https://newplayexchange.org/users/16975/alice-eve-cohen

EDISTO

Hal Corley

TATE, 20-year-old Virginia college sophomore and take-no-prisoners activist. Five days before Nixon's first draft lottery in 1969, TATE responds to a friend's loaded question about whether gays are barred from active duty in Vietnam.

TATE

Yeah, there's a question about "tendencies." I have a tendency to pick red onions out of tuna salad. A tendency to scream on roller coasters. Tendency to say, "fuck you" to war mongers talking about morality. I have a tendency to tell nosy childhood friends exactly what they want to know. *(Pause.)* I hear they send you to another floor in the induction center. Cubicle with no window. Little man with clammy hands and a bow tie and maybe a beatnik goatee with part of his breakfast stuck to it asks questions. "Have you tried to off yourself? Do you have anxiety?" — about anything besides having your dick blown off near the DMZ, they don't care about that. "Have you had gonorrhea? A homosexual experience? Shot heroin?" You can say, "Back up. That thing between the clap and smack. I did that, Doc." So you say, "When my girlfriend left me high n'dry I went to the Trailways station and got my manhood licked but good by a boy who looked like Sal Mineo. I liked it so much I went back the next morning. Again the next Sunday after Mass. Then stopped church and just lived at the Trailways. Now I can't remember what my girlfriend even looked like, but I could dig watching James Dean be nice to Sal Mineo in "Rebel Without a Cause" forever. Apparently if you confess that kinda experience, loaded with shame, they'll reject your trashy ass. But you have to be convincing. Stupid as they are, burnt out from dragging us into a fucking quagmire, they can smell a fake. Looks easy to pretend you're in the club, but the challenge is to be authentic. Not limp wrists. Or lisps. Lispers have a speech impediment, not the hots for other lispers. The *hots* aren't even it. It's not about blow jobs in tea rooms. Uh-uh. It's about — about negotiating the world. How you occupy the same space as other men. And knowing you're just as much a man as anyone else. Anyone. The shrink probably jerks off, soon as you leave. Letter arrives two weeks later, you're 4-F. *(Pause)* So. You're a grown-up. Fuckin' draftable. You could have your intestines splattered all over a rice paddy. End up face down in real mud, not the sand we pretended with playing war as kids. Start being who you are.

Information on this playwright may be found at
https://newplayexchange.org/users/3114/hal-corley

THE WONDERER

Lynda Crawford

WYNN, male, 50s+, is introducing himself to TRACEY, male or female, 30s+, who he meets on the ferry, even though TRACEY has been obviously trying to avoid conversation with him.

WYNN

Staten Island. Born and bred. These ferries are like my living room. I'm on 'em twice a day every day. Know all the regulars. Who likes to talk, who doesn't. Who's just ridin' for a place to flop. I watch out for the kids coming home from school. Make sure nobody's taking advantage of them. I make the rounds. Just my nature, I guess. And I can always spot the tourists. Most of 'em don't leave the terminal once we get to Staten Island. They just turn around and catch the next boat back to the city. I wish I could tell them to head out, walk around, take a bus ride to South Beach. Knew you weren't one of them. Not a tourist. And not a regular either. So I was just wondering … I was wondering … if you were one of them.

One of the jumpers.

Information on this playwright may be found at https://newplayexchange.org/users/6133/lynda-crawford

AGATHE

Angela J. Davis

In the following monologue, from AGATHE by Angela J. Davis, MBAYE, a Senegalese army captain on loan to a U.N. peace-keeping force, attempts to explain to North Americans a "kill sheet," a piece of paper listing names and families who will be slaughtered in a killing spree that the world will later recognize as the Rwandan genocide.

MBAYE

You call it "barbaric"?

No, no, no, no, no that's where ALL of you have it all wrong!

This is "evolved."

You want to see primitive "tribal warfare," go study the Anglo-Saxons and the French!

(indicating a paper sheet)

This, my friend, is an organized, "high volume" operation!

VERY twentieth-century!

That's one page out of tens of thousands.

All Tutsis. With their addresses.

Even the housekeepers for white missionaries!

And — you see, here?

The names of their wives!

Precise number and ages of the children.

(pointing)

These marks here, next to the number of family members?

That tells you: A woman in the household is expecting, so be sure to check for —

Catch your breath!

Listen to me!

This is their plan!

Pregnant women will be stabbed in the abdomen.

Teachers will kill their pupils. Doctors will kill their patients.

The priest will pull a dagger from his vestments.

The mayor, the music teacher, the mailman, the milk man —

ALL turn into home-made murderers! Overnight!

Nothing will be sacred.

Churches. Catholic girls' schools. Hospitals. Market stalls.

Public swimming pools, police headquarters, fishing docks, tennis courts, petrol stations, gymnasia —

ALL will turn into morgues.

Nothing and no one will be left out. Those who can't get their hands on a real weapon will be shown how to use their car rims and their farming implements —

Beating plowshares into swords.

And, my friend, they aim for Henry Ford efficiency —

Five hundred dead Tutsis every ten minutes.

They keep it going for just a few weeks, they surpass Hiroshima.

Information on this playwright may be found at https://angelajdavis.com

SENECA AND THE SOUL OF NERO

Marcia Eppich-Harris

NERO has been emperor for a number of years. Now, in his second marriage, his wife SABINA mourns the death of their child. She blames NERO for the child's death and wants to divorce him. In revenge for her threat of divorce, NERO kicks and beats SABINA to death. (She is also pregnant when she dies.) As she lies dead on the ground, NERO delivers the following monologue.

NERO

Why did you turn me into a monster, Sabina? Why? *(Screams)* I hate you.

Gods, what did I have to *fear* from you, Sabina? You could never tear your love away from me. Never. You were in a rage, and I — I could never meet fire with water, as Seneca always said. No. And now, who will avenge *you*? Who in Rome is brave enough to hold me to account? Who could judge me, sentence me to my doom? Who could examine the multitude of my sins? No one.

I shall have you mummified and keep you ever near me.

With your death, so dies Rome for me. I will return to Antium, the place of my birth. There, the world and I will mourn you, Sabina, and I shall see that Rome pays a price for your death.

Information on this playwright may be found at www.meppichharris.com

KARMA

Anne Flanagan

*CLERK, Officious and sarcastic, but highly efficient, CLERK
mans the desk of Purgatory (which resembles the DMV.) CLERK is
explaining to a newly deceased man what his future will look like in
the afterlife.*

CLERK

Yup, you're dead. I know, I know, there's supposed to be a tunnel and a white light but we had to cut all that, it's too expensive. Bummer, but welcome to Heaven! HA! Just kidding, Heaven doesn't exist. Sorry to break it to you. Actually, I'm not sorry — it's the best part of my job. B T dubs, there's no God, either, unless you count upper management.

What we DO have are varying qualities of afterlife, depending upon your placement. Think of it as an eternal cruise. The ship will provide for all your basic needs, my job is to determine the class in which you'll be traveling. That was, of course, a metaphor, which you'd understand had you completed undergrad. You know how they say, "No one's keeping score?" Guess what?! Someone is! They also say you can't take it with you, but you can, there's a loophole.

Anyhoo, someone IS keeping score; meticulously monitoring every moment of your life, comparing your data against others in the same demographic, which for you is White, Middle Class, American male. Childhood of moderate dysfunction. Now that you've shuffled off the mortal coil, my job is to compare your life with that of, say, your best friend from high school, Chaz Goldbaum. Same demographic, similar origins.

So. You, as an adult, were an underemployed web designer with vague aspirations of being a novelist. No wife, no kids, no property, etc., etc. Chaz, however, is an extremely successful producer/director with two adorable children and a lovely wife. Plus he drives a Bentley. Who wins? Psst, I'll give you a hint — it's not you.

Information on this playwright may be found at
https://www.anneflanagan.net

COUPLE OF THE CENTURY

William Ivor Fowkes

NICK TURNER, a 38-year-old college dropout from Flatbush, Brooklyn turned successful contractor. After hemming and hawing, NICK is finally explaining his problem to his therapist.

NICK

(NICK is seated in an armchair or on a sofa.) My wife doesn't like to have sex with me. I mean very often. Once every couple of weeks, maybe. *Maybe!* That's not normal, right? And then she acts like it took all her energy to accommodate me. Like she's done me this huge favor. Like New Year's Eve — the biggest night of the year, right? So, we pack the kids off to Grandma's. It was a perfect opportunity. Between the holidays and my flu and her colds, we hadn't made love for weeks, so I was really pent up. We went to an expensive restaurant and had a wonderful time.

So, what happens? We get home at two thirty and she falls right asleep. Now, I can understand that. The drinking. The late hour. OK, I get all that! But come morning, don't you think it's payback time? I mean, I was just looking forward to some good New Year's sex. Is that so wrong? And what happens? She can't even be bothered to brush her teeth, so we make love without any kissing. And I shouldn't even call it love. I mean, there wasn't any intercourse or anything — she said she wasn't in the mood — so instead she gives me a hand job. Thank you very much! Happy New Year to you, too!

But it's more than that. Even when she's in the mood, she's very limited in what she'll do. I like to try new things. She likes the same old routine. For instance, I like to start things standing up. I like to take it nice and slow. Explore a woman's body before jumping into bed. You know what I mean? But she insists on getting under the sheets right away. Says she gets cold, but that's not it. She's not cold. Well, she *is*, but … Anyway. One night I turned the heat up real high so no one could pretend they weren't comfortable and then made her stand up with me.

(He stands up.) We began to kiss, and I could already feel her tugging at me, trying to drag me back down to the bed, so I started to dance with her. *(He dances around the room.)* I waltzed her all around the room until I got her as far away from the bed as possible. Then I kissed her gently and massaged her shoulders, like it was our first time together. Like we were teenagers in love. And it was great! I got excited and hard as a rock. *(Looking down at himself.)* Who needs Viagra? This was the real thing! Then she says, "Oh, let's get back into bed, dear," but I hold on tight and try to persuade her to stay put.

"Baby, I'll do anything you want. Just tell me! Anything at all." And what does she do? She starts screaming her head off, pleading, saying she wants to get back into bed. So … I let her go. I didn't want to wake the kids. And that was it. *(He retakes his seat.)* The end of a great experiment!

Information on this playwright may be found at
https://newplayexchange.org/users/1077/william-ivor-fowkes

RUNTIME ERROR

Elana Gartner

TAL, a 21-year-old male Caucasian gay computer science student, opens the play with this direct address. He is struggling with the fact that he has been raped and betrayed by his male professor and mentor.

The stage is bare except for a solitary chair. The lighting is soft. TAL enters. He sits in the chair and tries to get comfortable. He squirms a bit, then starts squirming a lot. He starts breathing heavily and appears to be having a panic attack. He gets up and backs away from the chair. He leans over, trying to catch his breath. He looks up.

TAL

Oh, sorry, I'm just … I … the chair is not … *(Beat. HE looks up. Relenting)* Yeah, okay. *(He takes a deep breath and lets it out slowly. Beat. TAL nods and breathes again. Beat)* Um, could I … could I just sit on the floor? The chair is … I don't know … it's like squeaky and … I don't know … and the noise is just … you know … I mean, I can feel It in my chest, you know? *(Beat. TAL sits on the floor and tries to find a comfortable spot. He finally gets up and moves the chair away from him and sits back down again on the floor)* Okay, okay. I think I'm okay now. I think … yes. Sorry. *(Beat.)* Uhhh … yeah … a few times. *(Beat.)* I don't know. I don't know. I mean … I don't know. It's … uh … *(He looks around, uncomfortably)* I wish … I wish we got a blank slate … I mean, started with one, you know? Just started out … I don't know … clean … no baggage. *(Beat)* But we don't even really get a blank slate, do we? I mean … it's … *(Beat)* No, I'm not trying to distract … *(Sighing)* All right. Maybe I am. It's just … it's hard to … umm … Could we … umm … *(Beat)* Uh … okay. All right. I … ummm … well … I didn't exactly tell them when I figured it out … I mean … I sorta told them … they met Bruce, but they didn't really know … I mean, no one really did. My parents didn't talk about me a lot … it was

... I mean ... it was a lot about them ... And ... I don't know ... I just ... I tried to stay out of their way. Tried to ... you know ... not have them argue. Tried not to give them anything to argue about, especially me. I guess ... I just didn't have the space to be me until I got here, you know? It was just always about my parents and their fucking divorce. *(Beat)* I started programming because ... well, it was my escape from their insanity. They didn't really ... I mean, they didn't understand that I actually had skills until I got the scholarship to college. And I didn't even want ... my computer teacher told me that the way to convince my parents to let me go was to apply for the scholarship. I didn't want to. I hate ... I hate handouts. *(Beat)* Yeah, my computer teacher was great. I mean ... he gave me ... he gave me this book about ... machine learning and it was ... I mean, was written like ... um ... a long time ago ... back in the late 80's when neural networking was still becoming a thing. And I thought ... I thought this book was so incredible ... I mean, it was amazing, totally groundbreaking. Really simple title "What Is Machine Learning?" My teacher helped me find more books and papers by the guy. It was ... um ... by the time I was a senior ... I mean ... I knew more about this guy's theories than ... probably than I knew about my own parents ... that sounds weird but ... you know. *(Beat)* So I met him on a campus visit. He ... uh ... he was teaching a class. I got to ... I mean, I couldn't believe I got to sit in *his* class. I remember ... ummm ... I answered a question in that class. I, uh ... I probably wasn't ... you know ... I mean, I don't know if prospectives are supposed to participate ... but I could tell he ... ummm ... it sounds egotistical to say but, you know ... I knew what I was talking about. I knew what *he* was talking about. *(Beat)* He ... umm ... he signed my copy of the book I had with me that day ... it was a little embarrassing, but he was nice about it ... Programmers aren't usually known for their ummm ... for their social skills, you know ... but he was nice and ... uh ... funny, too. And engaging, you know? *(He looks down, sadly. Beat)*

Information on this playwright may be found at http://elanagartner.com/

THE OKTAVIST

Vince Gatton

DIMITRI, late teens/early-to-mid-20s. In a small church in Imperial Russia at the dawn of the 20th Century, Father Kirill has been approached by DIMITRI, the scion of a prominent local family, for a favor: the eager young man is convinced it's his divine calling to be an oktavist, one of the legendary ultra-deep-voiced singers in Russian liturgical music. After a brief audition, however, it's clear his voice is ridiculously too high to be an oktavist, no matter how fervent his belief. A disappointed DIMITRI explains to Father Kirill what led him to believe this impossible idea was not only possible, but an actual spiritual calling.

DIMITRI

I just … I know I'm very lucky. People tell me I'm very lucky and I am, I know that I am. But lately I've been feeling that, well, that a person has to have something more in his life — more than a wife and a, a, an income. One should have … a purpose. A passion.

Then yesterday as I sat listening to the choir, Andrei Volkov stepped out to sing … and I felt it *in my knees*. At the first notes, my knees suddenly became weak and tingly — I was lucky I was sitting down! And I studied his lips as they released that impossible sound, and his chest as it swelled with each breath, and the tingle went up the back of my neck — I shivered, I physically shivered! — and as my head rolled back my eyes looked up at the ceiling, at our beautiful, gilded ceiling, and I thought: how extraordinary! That this dark sound, which comes from such depths, can guide us up to the light, to the divine.

Such beauty. The sheer power of that beauty … it took my breath away. When he sings … the depth of it is … it's … well, in some ways it's terrifying, isn't it? And yet glorious? Like being given a small taste of what it would feel like to see the face of God: terrifying and glorious, all at once.

And that would have been the end of it, I suppose, but … but then, last night … I dreamed about it. About making that sound — that extraordinary, divine sound — myself. I dreamed that I was standing next to Andrei, here in St. Sophia, in front of everyone, as he began to sing. I stood there beside him, watching his face, his chest, his jaw, his lips, as he made that sound; and that sound, that vibration, entered into me, physically penetrated my body, and grew and grew until I too was making that sound, the vibrations building inside of me until they burst out, burst out like an explosion! An explosion of … of … of joy. A dark, deep, divine joy.

It felt like … ecstasy. An epiphany. It felt like … a calling.

So if you're saying it *wasn't* an epiphany … I don't … I don't know what it *was*.

Information on this playwright may be found at
https://newplayexchange.org/users/3190/vince-gatton

YEAR ONE

Erik Gernand

MAX, 30s-40s, a war veteran in 1933 Germany. MAX's sister recently discovered that he is part of an attempted assassination plot, and he must convince her of the evils of this new regime to enlist her assistance.

MAX

Katje and I were walking home from visiting friends near the park. We'd stopped going out to the queer clubs, it didn't feel safe anymore. We turned down a street and came upon this mass of young men. Teenagers. Younger than Peter, most of them. All wearing that brown uniform. It was actually, strangely, kind of beautiful. Nostalgic maybe. They were so enthusiastic. Singing. Marching. All together. You might think they were Scouts like in the old days. As we were walking away, a group of them approached us from behind. They had a question for Katje: Are you a man or a woman? But that's not what they really wanted to know. What they meant is are you an us or a them? When we divide, and that's what they're trying to do with all of us, where will you stand? Of course, the answer to their question didn't matter. They started hitting us. With fists. And sticks. And rocks. No matter how hard they hit, Katje got right back up. So, they hit harder and harder. When the police finally came, they laughed at her, ripped off her wig. They didn't want anything to do with me. It was crueler to separate us. So, they just took her. *(Beat.)* You would like Katje. I often think of you when I'm in an argument with her. She always wins too. I went to see her at the jail. They of course put her in a cell with men. The officer asked if I was her family. I don't know why I didn't say we were brothers. *(Beat. With newfound determination.)* I don't want your pity. I need you to help me end this.

Information on this playwright may be found at
http://www.erikgernand.com

MAN & WIFE

Emma Goldman-Sherman

RON is a manly Midwestern sports-fan, a red-blooded male not much older than his wife MISSY. He plays 29-54 in the play which spans 25 years. At this point, 25 years after 2016 (2041), RON has put on weight. He's wearing an ugly Christmas sweater, and he and his wife have just finished taping their holiday vlog for their relatives. RON is a laid-off commercial airline pilot who flew for the Marines in Iraq. They have two children, Sport and Sweetie (now both named Sam) who are both gender dysphoric, now trans female and nonbinary. Now RON and Missy are gently arguing about the election that took place a few months after they were married. Missy and RON have never discussed how he voted during the 2016 election although Missy (voted blue for the first time, for Hillary) has been suspicious of RON for the past 25 years. It has come up again, and this time she is going to let him tell her the truth because he says he voted with her in mind, and for the first time in 25 years she is able to listen.

RON

Do you remember the week before the election? The first of November was a Tuesday, it was hot as hell, broke records, in the 80s all across the Midwest, and I was late to a doctor's appointment with you. He didn't look like a baby then, he looked like a space ship. And I couldn't believe I'd be a dad, but we did it. Do you remember the second day of November? The Cubs beat the Indians and won the World Series after losing for a hundred and eight years. I realized that anything in the world was possible. Then the day before the election, Leonard Cohen died — don't interrupt me — Leonard Cohen died — made me feel as if I had something important to do in this world, that there was holiness to be found somewhere if I looked for it, and I looked for it, and I found you sleeping beside me. The night before the election, you went to bed early exhausted, you said you felt like a factory, as if you were literally making our child out of parts on some inner assembly line with a deadline to meet, and all I wanted was to make something wonderful with you, and that something wonderful would be called our life together, our family, our lives, to be safe in a special place where nothing could get to us. There was this woman running for office talking in every debate about a No-Fly Zone. I used to watch a lot of C-Span, and I saw General Dunford, my old boss, the Commandant of the Marine Corps, he was asked what it would mean to have a No-Fly Zone over Syria. He was very clear — my commanding officer — he said very clearly, "Senators, that would mean war for us against Russia, war." I didn't know if our child would be a boy or a girl. I didn't know there were other options. And I didn't want war with Russia. So I voted with my heart to keep my family safe. I would like to wake up beside you and know that you love me. Do you want me to go?

Information on this playwright may be found at
https://newplayexchange.org/users/1088/emma-goldman-sherman

FRAGILE

Dana Leslie Goldstein

RENNIE, late 20s-early 30s, African American or multi-racial ethnicity, Proprietor of Infinity Flux Comics. RENNIE is about to lose his beloved comic book shop. When Alana walks into the store and says she's interested in buying the building, something doesn't seem right. Then, thinking she's helping, she criticizes his business skills.

RENNIE

I'm not interested in being a salesman. I'm honest. And I don't like being beholden to anyone. I don't like not knowing what's going on around me. Or what my relationship is to something — or someone. I usually have a really good sense of that kind of thing. And yeah. It's a superpower. It's helped keep me alive. Through some pretty tough times.

What's going on here? I woke up this morning with a funny feeling — a feeling like something was about to shift. And then you walked in here — and everything did. I hate the idea of losing this store because the building gets sold. But I understand it. It's fucking capitalism. It's why I'd rather tell you to come back in two months for the book you actually want, even if my store isn't here at that point, than hide it from you. Lie to you. Not saying is also lying. You don't know anything about comics. Why would you even want to buy this building? All you know is the business part, which is shitty by definition — Unless — *(stopping himself)* Who are you, really? Are you actually some huge creator or something — that's why you look familiar — and this is going to be a pet project? You are, aren't you? I should've known. Something's fishy when a Black woman hasn't heard of Storm.

Information on this playwright may be found at
https://danalesliegoldstein.com

BEFORE YOU GET MARRIED

Franky D. Gonzalez

JASON, 28, reveals to his sister ALICIA, 24, that he's suspected not being related to his sister for years after ALICIA, claims that their deceased mother left behind a recording on a cassette declaring the siblings to not be blood related.

JASON

I don't remember Mom being pregnant. I don't remember Dad. I just remember … one day, you were there. I didn't think about it. I was four and had a baby sister. I forgot. But I think I knew. I never said anything. What would happen if I told everyone I thought you weren't my sister? Or what would everyone think of Mom? Would Mom deny it? Would she make up some story about how she got us? Would she mention two men, or something else? Why didn't she bring it up? I suspected something, but if Mom never said anything, then I could play stupid. *(Silence.)* It hurts. Watching someone grow up, and they're not … they're not what you thought. But it's not true you tell yourself. It's not true and she's still the same, no matter what. *(Silence.)* And like nothing. Mom dies. You're 17 and I'm 21. I find the package with all the stuff she left behind. It says that it's for us. Her dear children. And I knew. I knew the truth was in there. Jesus, come on. How in the hell can I go on thinking that we're related? All I needed to do was listen to the tape and confirm it. But I didn't. I held onto the package. *(Pause.)* I was afraid. I wanted to know. I wanted to confirm the truth. But I delayed it. Why should I let what we have end? Why should the truth come out so soon? So, I held onto it for a few years longer. Promising myself each year that I'd give it to you this time around. But I didn't. And now, you're 24 and about to get married. It was now or never. So, I made up some bullshit story about me finding it with Mom's stuff and … here we are.

Information on this playwright may be found at
https://newplayexchange.org/users/6600/franky-gonzalez

SHYLOCK THE FIRST

Andrew R. Heinze

SHAKESPEARE, 34, addresses his beloved protégé, WILL HATCHER, 21, a young actor whom SHAKESPEARE has cast to play Shylock in the very first production of The Merchant of Venice. WILL has been pressing SHAKESPEARE to add more lines to round out Shylock, a demand SHAKESPEARE consistently refuses. Finally WILL quits the company. SHAKESPEARE wants him back.

SHAKESPEARE

You insist on more. He insists on more. Here you are, an actor, a player on my stage. Here am I, your author, the one who gives you your livelihood, your vocation, the platform for your art, the one who gives you, in sum, something to do in this world. Yet you stand there, a young whelp barely out of his teens, you stand there and insist. You insist you know better than I whether you need more. You insist! You will be the judge, the arbiter and accountant of my words. You stand there, brazenly bold, and insist. You insist? Without my words what are you, Will? Without my words, you are mute. Without my words, you are null, you are nil, you are not. Without my words … *(pause, gentles his tone)* Will. Will. Come back to me. You cannot leave me like this. We open tomorrow. An actor, an actor must have a spine. *(pause, then responding to a retort)* What's that you say? You have spine enough for us both? Ah, a double-spined man, a miracle of nature! All hail, Lord Cartilage, who makes cartilaginous cowards of us all. *(pause, then responding to a retort)* And what's this you say? You have suffered my abuse long enough? You? You have suffered? You suffer the suffering of the pampered child, feeling himself always let down, and let down all the more the more he is given. You were fifteen when I took you under my wing. Six years of care I have given you, care almost maternal, as if I were not only woman-born but born a woman. That is the quality of my tenderness for you. Tenderness only, tenderness always, for you. That is the reason behind your complaint. Too much tenderness. I tended you in the garden of theater and in that soil you flourished. You, who had intellect enough for any vocation; you, who had beauty enough for Socrates. You had all this and not only all this but also the gift of an actor. That gift, which has the heavenly power to move men and women from trouble to joy, dullness to wonder, smugness to sympathy, that gift you are now delighted to leave in the dirt, to renounce, to quit. After all I've done for you, this is your repayment? this is my remuneration? A swift exit, with neither wave goodbye nor word of thanks? *(pause)* You owe me, but more than that: you owe yourself. To see you run away from a part? It is not credible, it is not laudable, it is not suitable to a man of your quality. *(brief pause)* Think for a moment. Think. Consider. *(pause)* Come back with me. We must have you. I must have you.

Information on this playwright may be found at https://andrewheinze.com

BEST LAID PLANT(T)S

Donna Hoke

BENNETT, a mid-thirties male, finally breaks free of an abusive relationship in front of the best friend he has unrecognized feelings for.

BENNETT

I didn't make the choice the first time, Nina. You did. You chose to walk out. You made every choice. You chose the food and the wine and the position and the location and the reasons I should forgive you and when I tried to choose something, I chose one thing. I chose this couch and I think — I think this couch, this choice, might be — is — the best choice I ever made in my life.

You chose to walk out and now you think you can choose to walk back in. It's not a choice, Nina, but if it were, I don't choose you. I choose my friend. I choose myself. I choose my life. Most of all I choose this fucking couch. Again. And if you burn it down, AND IF YOU BURN IT DOWN AGAIN, I will choose it again. And again and again and again and again. Forever. I love this couch!

Information on this playwright may be found at https://newplayexchange.org/users/253/donna-hoke

BRILLIANT WORKS OF ART

Donna Hoke

JAMES, 25, an artist tells a rich and refined prospective buyer how he discovered his place in his family.

JAMES

Uh, okay. It's summer. My brother is at some sports camp, my parents want to take a vacation. The most dangerous thing my father thinks I might do is hit my head coming out of the closet, so they leave me home. Alone. Uninterrupted alone. All I want to do is draw — the couch, my knee, the trees outside, this basket of flowers on the mantle. They're silk, but they look real, blooming eternally in shades of russet, wee bits of orange, gold. Suddenly, I notice the wallpaper has the thinnest of gold stripes. I'd never noticed them before. It's the flowers that have made them emerge. Pop. The more I look around the room, the more I notice things like this. I'm fucking — excuse me — I'm fucking gobsmacked! My mother had *designed* this room. With very little money. I … I lit up. I wasn't alone in this family. Not a freak. Not even an accident. My father might never understand me, but I belonged to my mother.

Information on this playwright may be found at https://newplayexchange.org/users/253/donna-hoke

THE EARLY MIRACLE

Lew Holton

JUNIOR enters, dressed all in black. He approached the mobile home of JANET SUE ATKINS — the only mobile home that survived a tornado touchdown in the Fairview Trailer Park in the town of Early, South Carolina. He carries a dog's food bowl filled with dog food, an empty water bowl, and a can of beer. A towel is draped around his neck.

JUNIOR

(Calling) Ace! Gene! Here, boys! *(He looks off, listens.)* Cold beer and Kibbles, boys! *(He sets the food bowl and the water bowl on the ground. He opens the beer, takes a sip, and holds it up.)* Ice cold, boys! Gene! Ace! *(He sighs, pours the beer into the water bowl, then speaks to unseen JANET SUE who has come to her door in response to his calls.)* Oh, hey. It's just me — Junior. From next door. USED to be next door ... I'm sorry to bother you. I wanted to ask you a favor. ... You know Ace and Gene're still missin'. Well ... I was just thinkin'. If they do try to come home, we wouldn't be here — with our place gone an' all, I mean. So I was just wondrin' if I could leave their food dish an' all over here at your place? ... I mean, you hear 'bout these things all the time, ya know. Like that Disney movie — animals travelin' from way off somewhere to get back home. It's like they have this special sense or somethin'. Like a built-in compass. An' they cross mountains an' rivers an' hitch rides on trucks an' stuff to get back to their families ... So I was just thinkin' — what if they do all that an' make it all the way back here an' what they see is ... nothin'? 'Cause ever'thing's gone, I mean. Except your place. So I thought if they saw their food bowl, they'd know we hadn't forgot 'em. That we hadn't just took off an' left 'em, ya know? *(He takes the towel from his neck.)* I been carryin' this around with me a couple of days. June an' me slept with it last night so it'd have our scent on it. I thought I'd leave it with their food bowl. If it's okay with you, I mean ... June an' me're

stayin' over at her sister's place for right now. I could leave you her number. In case they show up, ya know … Boy, you really lucked out, huh? The tornado thing an' all, I mean. We been readin' 'bout you in those supermarket papers an' all. Talkin' about a miracle and folks comin' here to pray an' all. That's really somethin'. I mean, I never thought you were, like, real religious or anything. It's kinda weird, ya gotta admit … So I was just thinkin' … you been doin' any prayin' or anything since it happened? 'Cause I was just wonderin' that, if you had been, an' if you maybe had some kinda inside track or somethin' — well … maybe you'd put in a good word for Ace an' Gene, ya know? I'm not askin' for myself, really. Hell, they're just dogs, ya know? But they never hurt nobody. They don't deserve this. I mean, I know the mailman was scared of 'em, an' we had to get a box down at the post office 'cause he didn't wanna deliver the mail here, but all they ever did was bark at him. They never hurt nobody … Anyway — I wouldn't ask you to do nothin' you weren't comfortable with, but I just thought I'd ask. 'Cause, ya know, even if that damn twister got 'em — I mean, even if they got hurt so bad they ain't never comin' back, you'd think somebody woulda at least found 'em an' called or somethin'. That way, we could at least give 'em … a decent burial, ya know? They deserve that at least, don't they? *(He takes a piece of paper from his pocket.)* I wrote down the number for June's sister. Just in case, ya know? An' I 'preciate it. Me an' June both really 'preciate it. *(Lights fade to black.)*

Information on this playwright may be found at
https://lewholton.squarespace.com/

PATIENCE AND FORTITUDE

Arlene Hutton

REG, male, 21, a not-very-serious college business major, finds himself stranded for days in a house with eight other college students. The internet is down, the electricity is off and there's a big snowstorm. Fear brings out the worst in people and REG is fed up with the group dynamic.

REG

You know, I'm really tired of you making assumptions about me. *(He looks at each of them.)* Yeah, you do. All of you. You think because I'm in a fraternity I'm a certain way. You think I get drunk and drive fast. You all think that I'm dumb because I'm not artsy. Or into social issues. Like because I'm in business I'm dumb. You think you have all the answers. You pretend to be open and accepting, and you welcome, what, diversity, but you're really a bunch of hypocrites. *(He doesn't give anyone time to answer.)* You're biased against me because I look the way I do and I dress the way I do. You think anyone who has money is bad and then you totally depend on people like my family to give money to you so you can think you're saving the world or make your stupid art. And what you don't know is that my dad's father was disowned by his family before I was born and we don't have any money, never had any money, but you think I do because I'm in a fraternity. *(He looks at them one by one.)* I'm on scholarship. I get my clothes at thrift stores and used online, or they're hand-me-downs from my cousin who feels sorry for me. You've all been making assumptions about me because of my taste in clothes and the friends I hang out with and the way I look. Aren't you ashamed of yourselves now?

Information on this playwright may be found at arlenehutton.com

I NAME YOU

Rebecca Kane

CHRIS, a frat boy, has been kidnapped and tortured by two teenage girls who believe he raped someone close to them. With a pair of pliers at his face, he's ordered to tell the truth.

CHRIS

She said I was cute. She went back to my room with me and everything. She sat on my bed, even. Why would she sit on my bed if she didn't want to do anything? She came in, and she sat and leaned back all relaxed, not looking at me, she's on her phone. She sat there and she kept scrolling through her phone. I was trying to talk to her but she wasn't saying much. I asked about her friends and what her major was but she just sort of gave yes or no answers to everything. I didn't think she didn't WANT to be there, she just seemed nervous. Lots of girls get nervous before hooking up. She said, "I should go." But I thought it was just because maybe she wasn't having fun so I made a joke about it, you know, I said she shouldn't worry, we were going to have fun. I thought I'd make her less nervous, show her it was okay, and I was interested in her, and we were gonna have fun!, so I took her phone and put it down for her. Then we kissed. I kissed her, she didn't push me away. She sort of responded. I pushed her back on the bed, but I didn't really push, I mean, she leaned back, and I followed her. She reached for her phone, I just wanted to make sure it wouldn't get lost in the bed, you know, and so we both knew where it was, when she picked up her phone, I took it out of her hand and put it on the desk. It was totally within reach! And I didn't like, force it away, I just sort of took it from her and put it down, so we wouldn't have to worry. And then we kept making out. She wasn't doing much. She said, "Where's your roommate?" and I thought, oh, she's finally getting into it, she's worried we're gonna get interrupted, so I told her not to worry, I got up, and locked the door. Then I went back to her and we kept going and that's it! We had sex! I asked her, the whole time I kept asking her over and over and over if she was okay. Every time she said yes. Any of those times, she could have said no. If she had just said no.

Information on this playwright may be found at
https://newplayexchange.org/users/16500/rebecca-kane

CLEAR BLUE SKY

Bruce Karp

HARVEY — a 40-year-old man working for a security company in Southern Maine. He was on duty at the Portland Airport's security kiosk the morning of 9/11, and he is explaining what happened that morning to his boss, who didn't know he played a role in that day's tragic attacks.

HARVEY

An explanation.

(Pauses, to collect thoughts)

Okay, here it is … in a nutshell.

(Gets increasingly upset as he tells the story)

An enterprising reporter for our local paper decided to start asking around to find out who was on duty the morning of 9/11 at the Portland airport, and let the terrorists get past the security check. Someone kindly gave him my phone number, so he called me, I told him my story, my feelings of shame, regret, remorse, and they published it, leaving out the part about my feelings, making it sound as if I were treating it as no big deal, because I laughed once, out of nervousness. I became an instant sensation, the devil incarnate, which led to death threats, a broken windshield on my car, a break-in at my apartment … basically, a scarlet letter was applied to my forehead. I lost my job, was unemployed for months, my family and the people who I thought were my friends wouldn't talk to me. No one wanted to hear my side of the story, nor did they care. I was the guy who let the terrorists into the country on 9/11. It took a good couple of years before I could even begin to stabilize my life. Even now, I still can't face September 11th when it rolls around each year. I still feel the shame and the guilt. This past 9/11, they reprinted the article from 2001 in the local paper, so I got to see it rehashed all over again. Guess you didn't see it. Don't you think it's kind of ironic that someone who supposedly allowed the worst security breach in the country's history now works for a security company?

(He starts laughing.)

Information on this playwright may be found at
https://newplayexchange.org/users/1828/bruce-karp

FLAWLESS

Davida Kilgore

CHARLES a 50-year-old, white man, married to a 42-year-old Black American woman. He is talking to his wife following her disclosure that she once had an affair with a woman.

CHARLES

(resigned) What am I supposed to do with what you've told me? How can I believe that you won't leave me if … let me finish. How can I believe that you won't leave me if you ever find her, wherever she is? Whoever she is? Your words. I feel like you settled for me, because … because I don't know why? *(anger finally coming out)* Just to be married. To have children. You didn't have to be with me just for that. And all the time I thought you were having blips of moments because I'm white. You were having those thoughts because I'm a man. You love women. Yes, there's that word again: love. I'm beginning to think like you, that it doesn't mean anything, a reaction to an action. Me, giving you all of me and you needing more than I am capable of giving because I am a man. Damnit, Angi, why didn't you tell me this before today, before the marriage, before Von and Noni? Why didn't you just tell me, maybe we would have stayed together, maybe not? It's too late now, and it's never too late. What are you saying? … If we're going to stay together that will have to be enough. You have to give me a moment to digest all of this, all of you. Angi, I love you, but right now I'm disappointed. You didn't give me a chance, you didn't trust me enough to share all of who you are. Not even during counseling when we were getting everything out in the open about our feelings toward each other. Truth, remember. Truth.

Information on this playwright may be found at www.davidakilgore.com

YOU BELONG TO ME

Debbie Lamedman

YOUNG MAN, any race or ethnicity, late teens, early 20s, talks directly to the audience about his boyfriend, and whether or not their relationship may be abusive. This piece appears as an Interlude between scenes in the play.

YOUNG MAN

He tells me he loves me and I believe him. I love him too. This relationship is what I've always wanted. We're both out and proud of it. He's very romantic. He holds my hand all the time. Wherever we go … he holds my hand. Lately, he's been correcting my grammar. So weird. But kinda funny. When I laugh at him for doing it, he gets mad. He's also begun to criticize the way I dress. He used to compliment me all the time. Said I was a "sharp dresser." Now he's telling me I look awful. If I get upset, he says I'm too sensitive. Last week we went to a party. Whenever I talked to other people, he told me to stop ignoring *him*. He's accusing me of cheating on him. I'm not. Not at all. He gets so jealous if I talk to anyone who's not him. He said, "I don't like it when you look at other guys. I only want you to look at me." What am I supposed to do? Walk around with blinders on? He doesn't want me to go anywhere without him. If I want to get a cup of coffee without him, he immediately has a meltdown and says I don't love him and he'll never be able to live without me. I'm feeling suffocated. Trapped. I'm thinking about breaking up with him. He knows I'm pulling away. But he makes threats that if I leave him, he'll kill himself. I said, "No you won't. You'll be fine." And he said, "Are you testing me? Do you want to find out if I'll actually do it? How could you live with yourself if I died because you left me? What kind of person are you?"

I don't know what to do. I feel like I'm being held hostage by my own boyfriend.

Information on this playwright may be found at https://www.debbielamedman.com/

ASSUMPTIONS

Eric Lane

RAY, teens to early 30s, a keen mind though not intellectual. Direct. As RAY and Bailey (older) work, they discuss various subjects ranging from whether Shakespeare was depressed when he wrote "Hamlet" to the danger of making assumptions. After Bailey speaks theoretically about RAY'S father who is deceased, RAY surprises him.

RAY

I thought I saw him.

My father. Felt him anyway. Yesterday I'm writing about him. Who he was. At least to me. Some of it happy. Some, not so much, you know. And just when I get to the end, it starts to erase. The words on the screen. Letters. Disappear, starting at the end and heading to the top. Letters. Words. Sentences. Getting eaten and there's nothing I can do to stop it. Each line. Each memory. Gone.

I'm thinking it's my dad come back. That he hates what I'm writing and is erasing it 'cause it's just not true. It fuckin' scares the shit outta me, 'til I realize it's not him, it's me. My second keyboard. I keep a second keyboard attached to my laptop in case I wanna type on my lap. The keys are bigger and I have it leaning against my desk. My leg accidentally pressed against it. Against the 'Delete' button. Me thinking it's some great message from the beyond. Some fuckin' Twilight Zone moment of connection, but it's just my leg.

[Bailey laughs slightly.]

Right.

Information on this playwright may be found at http://www.ericlanewrites.com/

GETTING BACK SHANTEL

Drew Larimore

RANDY, a 20-something novice YouTube rapper, stands outside an apartment door.

He bangs on it. Nothing. He waits, shifting his weight. He bangs on the door again. Still nothing. He bangs furiously a third time with both fists. Beat. Nothing.

RANDY

(to the door)

Shantel, I ...

(Beat)

Yo, I brought you some cookies.

(Beat)

Peanut butter. They melt in your mouth — not in your ...

(Suddenly embarrassed, he looks away.)

Shit.

(A longer pause. He sighs, setting his head against the door.)

I bombed tonight. The Apollo. I got out there and didn't say nothin'— no rhymes, no raps — bombed, you hear me? I ran outta there as fast as I could. I had hundreds-a-people there for me and all I did was just stand there like — like some playa.

(Beat.)

You gotta understand, Shantel, I — I freaked out when I was over here last. The whole thing, you gotta admit — the whole thing's mad scary. I mean, I've been tryin' to make sense of it in my head and everythin's been so confused up in there that I haven't been able to sleep or eat right and — look, I just wanna see you. Can you open the door? Please?

(Beat; nothing.)

I wanna say I'm sorry for talking to you like that. You didn't deserve it. And even though I wished you had told me sooner … I guess I know why you didn't.

(Beat)

Look, I know you gotta dick. And you know I gotta dick. We've both got ourselves dicks here and Shantel, there's a lot I don't understand. Like, how long have you been like this, when did you know you were really — you know, if you played football or shit in school and if you sit or stand when you take a piss. But listen, ever since you walked into my life, my life's been diff'rent. And I dunno if you havin' a dick's got anything to do with that and the more I think about it, the more I don't care. I just care about you.

(Beat.)

You make me sing, Shantel. You make me better.

(Pause. He leans his head against the door. Downtrodden. He bends down, picking up the destroyed box.)

I'm leavin' you the cookies. In case you're hungry?

(Beat. He knocks lightly a final time.)

'Night.

Information on this playwright may be found at https://drewlarimore.com/

THE KISS

Lee Richard Lawing

TONY, an 80-year man who was in the Korean War where he experienced his first kiss with another man whose name was Chip. TONY is now married to Chip who has Alzheimer's and does not remember or recognize TONY any longer.

TONY

Here's another picture of you that I loved from then. You're in the sun on board the ship. There's that entire book of men aboard ship during the war and I always thought I should have sent them yours to include.

But I know you're not flashy like that. Not into making the world aware of you.

But I was and still am.

I hate that you're not here with me anymore, the way we had planned. But no one can really plan anything can they? No one can make such promises that extend too far into the future when there's such blackness that steals so much from you.

It's stolen you from me, but I will sit here, and I will watch over you until you're completely gone because I promised you I would. As hard it is, I will stay with you until you close your eyes forever.

I like it best when you sleep because I can still kiss you then. I guess some might think that wrong of me. Kissing you when you don't truly remember me, or recognize me, but to them I say try spending 60 plus years with someone and not want to try to still kiss them.

When you like that sort of thing. And I always did.

(TONY sits beside CHIP and he takes up CHIP's hand and he kisses it gently.)

And I always will till either of us can't run anymore.

Information on this playwright may be found at https://newplayexchange.org/users/20860/lee-r-lawing

POST-MORTEM

David Lewison

A hospital waiting room. MAX, a grieving man in his 80s, speaking to the young doctor who has come out to console him just minutes after MAX'S wife has passed away.

MAX

This isn't about me being upset, doctor. This is about me being honest for the first time in fifty years. Now that she's gone. I hated my wife. Because she hated me. Oh, we had some good times together at first. But nothing I ever did was good enough for her. The job I had, the money I made, the home we lived in. Every day, from morning to night, she nagged and yelled and complained. I got insomnia from her pestering me at night, and ulcers from her yelling at me during the day.

Thank God I had my work at least. At work, I could be away from her for ten hours a day and be respected for what I was. A man among men. But at home, my life was hell. And there was always so much pressure on us to stay together. First from our friends and our families, then from our kids and our grandchildren. They all saw what it was like. They all saw we hated each other. But it was never convenient for them, for us to be apart.

So for them, we stayed together. We never even talked about divorce, not even once. I see other people in this life, other couples, and they seem to be happy with each other. That wasn't what it was like for us. For us, it was constant misery and suffering. But at least it's finished now. It's finished now for both of us. I have a chance now to start over again. I know I'm not young anymore. I'm not even old anymore. I'm ancient. Who knows how long I'm gonna live myself? But at least I have a chance now, for as long as I've got. A chance to live a life again. There's just one problem …

(MAX pauses, then bursts into tears.)

I miss her so much ...

(MAX stares forward, continuing to grieve, as the LIGHTS DIM ...)

Information on this playwright may be found at
http://davidlewison.com/

THE BOOTH

David Lewison

The projection booth inside a seedy, decaying movie theater in the mid-1980's. A dull, continuous roar from the off-stage film projectors. Just barely audible at times, the heavy MOANING from the soundtrack to a hardcore porno film. MARTIN, 50s, the owner, is addressing the theater's just-hired projectionist.

MARTIN

Everything going okay up here? What's the matter? You shocked? Offended? Don't worry, kid, you'll do fine. Now remember, you got three complete features here. Run 'em straight through, back-to-back, without stopping. If you can keep the reels in order, that's a plus, but always have something on screen. And never bring up the houselights before closing. Believe me, you don't want to see what's going on in there. So let me guess, you're going to college, right? A college boy. Going to make something of your life. Yeah, what a crock of shit that is. What are you studying? No, I bet I already know. Movies, right? Except you call it filmmaking, or cinema, or some kind of bullshit like that ... mind if I smoke?

(Not waiting for a reply, MARTIN goes ahead and lights up.)

I tell you, the golden age of this side of the business is over. Used to be there were adult movie theaters all over the city, every neighborhood, practically. Now it's just down to a few. All my life I wanted to own a place like this, and now I can barely keep it afloat. And what about these movies they keep sending me? You call that acting? Directing? Cinematography? You're the budding Cecil B. DeMille here, what do you think? They're nothing, nothing but crap. Because they aren't thinking about the big screen anymore, just how it'll play on video. The tits are still big, but the movies have gotten small. Hell, even that's not really true, most of these chicks today get so pumped up full of silicone they probably constitute a fire hazard ...

(He pauses, taking a drag on his cigarette.)

Now it was different in the old days, ten, twenty years ago. The Sixties and the Seventies. They had real bodies then. Yeah, they'd pull some hippie chick in off the street, lay some bread on her, and boom, there it was. Sweet and natural. You know who could do that now, really make some good money? Tina. You saw her downstairs, the chick in the box office. She's my niece, lives with me in my apartment over on Las Palmas. Yeah, she's got a hot little body on her. I even tried introducing her to some producers I know. I mean, really legitimate people, with offices in Northridge and everything. But she wasn't interested. Fucking kids today, they don't have any ambition. And let me tell you, it isn't easy having her flouncing around my place half-naked all the time. I mean, that's what she calls me, Uncle Marty. But she's really just a stepniece, related by marriage. Yeah, no problem there. Not one bit. I wouldn't mind giving it to her twenty ways before breakfast one of these days …

(He pauses, looks at the projectionist.)

What's wrong now? You think you're too good for this, college boy? Well, fuck you. Go ahead and leave. You probably don't even need the fucking money —

(Relenting, MARTIN holds up his hand.)

Wait. Wait a minute. Look, I don't want to have to put another want ad in the goddamn Recycler. So this isn't exactly your dream job. I'll up your pay to nine dollars an hour. No, make it ten. What do you say?

(Off his hesitation.)

You know, I know some people who could help you get into the business. And hey, maybe you'll hit it off with Tina, she likes smart kids like you. Come on. What do you say?

(MARTIN smiles at his response.)

Good decision. Don't worry, kid. Like I said, you'll do fine. We're like family here. Tell you what, I'll send up Tina with some popcorn for you later …

(About to exit, MARTIN turns to look at him.)

You touch her, I'll fucking break your neck, you understand?

(Not waiting for a reply, MARTIN is out the door. The sounds of heavy moaning from the film sound track increase. LIGHTS FADE.)

Information on this playwright may be found at
http://davidlewison.com/

FERGUSON

Joan Lipkin

MATT, a young gay male in his early twenties to late thirties who sells skincare products and makeup at Sephora and loves pop culture, partner to Chad. They are in their apartment, having an argument about going to a Black Lives Matter protest. Chad wants to go. MATT doesn't want to and is trying to make Chad understand why.

MATT

(to CHAD) Are you seriously going to lecture me about oppression, Chad? Seriously? Given that I grew up in Bumfuck, Texas, and my parents dragged my queer teenage ass to some fucking ministry because I liked pretty? Because I wanted to be pretty, because I just wanted to ... be. I mean, really? What I understand is that these fucking protesters don't give a rat's ass about anyone. They shut down the highway. The fucking highway. How are people supposed to go to work? What if someone needs to get to the hospital? You know, like when Donny did. It's inconvenient. It's rude. It's inconsiderate, and frankly, I'm sick of it. It's all anyone talks about anymore. It's dividing our friends. It's dividing us. Why are you so invested in this? It's not that I don't care. I do. But I don't agree with these tactics. They just seem wrong. I'm sorry. But this does not seem like the way to gain allies. And you know, sometimes, I just want to go to my job, come home to my boyfriend on a Friday night after a tough week, watch some stupid television, walk the dog, get laid. You know, the American Dream. If that makes me superficial, okay, then I'm superficial.

Information on this playwright may be found at https://newplayexchange.org/users/63172/joan-lipkin

OF NIGHT SHADOWS

John Mabey

ANGUS, a man, any adult age. He is speaking to his wife, motioning outside their window at a shadow on the sidewalk down below. He's pleading with her to stay as he confesses to a crime where he struck a stranger with his car and buried the body in the desert. This accident occurred at 3 AM and now every night at 3 AM he sees the shadow outside.

ANGUS

Do you see? Look! Down there.

Every night at 3 AM. Always in shadows. His gets longer as he passes under the streetlight, hat pulled down. And just when he's beyond the light, I see his shadow stop. And turn. To look at me — through me. Disconnected, angry.

Don't leave me, please. I'll go to the police. I'll confess.

Bodies are heavy. A man 170 pounds will carry as 200 pounds easy. Like a magic trick. No one is supposed to be that color. I read at the library how it's a sign of internal bleeding. And how head wounds might only give the appearance of death. I'm no doctor — how was I to know? Because if I did, I would've taken him to a hospital — only a monster would do the opposite. But then he opens his eyes, already deep in the hole. Face coved in dirt. Eyes looking straight at me — through me — as I held the shovel. Tell me, what was I supposed to do?

I don't know the word — the one he screamed. Maybe it was his name. Maybe my name. Maybe in that moment he knew everything there was to know. You think I'm going mad. But what if it's him? Out there. Waiting.

Do you see?

Information on this playwright may be found at https://mabeyplays.com/

SHERLOCK HOLMES AND THE ADVENTURE OF THE FALLEN SOUFFLÉ

David MacGregor

AUGUSTE ESCOFFIER is the most famous chef in the world. Facing ruin, scandal, and possible assassination, both he and Bertie, the Prince of Wales (the future King Edward VII of England), have come to the rooms of Sherlock Holmes for help. In this scene, ESCOFFIER has prepared a gourmet treat for the gluttonous Bertie, as Sherlock Holmes, Dr. Watson, and Irene Adler look on in bewilderment.

ESCOFFIER

My friends, please allow me to present to you the rarest dish in the world. Delicate, sublime, illegal in many countries, yes, but a favorite of His Royal Highness when it can be procured on the black market. But first, I shall place a clean linen napkin over the head of His Royal Highness — patience my good sir, let the anticipation build — because the napkin will help to retain the aromas of the dish once it is uncovered … and also, so they say, assist in hiding one's shame from God.

You may well wonder what this is dish is called, and so I shall tell you. It is ortolan. A tiny, delicate, beautiful little songbird … no larger than my thumb. Caught in nets, they are kept in total darkness so they overeat, and then they are drowned in a vat of Armagnac brandy, then roasted whole. You uncover the dish … take in the intoxicating scent … and then place the entire bird in your mouth.

When you bite down you hear the crunch of the bones and feel the hot flesh and innards sliding down your throat. You chew slowly, grinding the skin, the bones pricking the inside of your cheeks so that your own warm blood mingles with the fat that tastes of hazelnuts. And now, Your Royal Highness, bon appétit!

Information on this playwright may be found at https://www.david-macgregor.com

I'LL CALL YOU MINE

Ali MacLean

PAUL, early 30s, a smart, embittered bar manager who never quite got over breaking up with his high school sweetheart MOLLY, is in the flower shop with his newish girlfriend EMILY 40s. EMILY has been talking about the vacation they are supposed to take together. PAUL has been looking for a way to let her down gently. Or not.

PAUL

Look. The thing about Molly? When Molly left for college it's like my molecules changed. My body actually changed. I felt like I was going to die. You know scientists have proved that 'heartache' isn't just an expression, it's an actual physical sensation. An ailment. And it's true. I was physically sick for a year. I had to go on disability. And it wasn't depression. It wasn't just a sad feeling that made it hard for me to fall asleep or the feeling like I couldn't get out of bed. I had that too. I had, you know, that post-break-up bullshit of not wanting to shower or answer the phone. Or trying to eat food, but everything you put in your mouth tastes like sand the moment it hits your tongue. Or feeling lonely when you're with a crowd of people. And then there were the girls. Fucking dozens of random girls. Trying to somehow connect with them but you can't so you end up just stabbing them with your cock, just to feel something. And then you feel even less the moment you come. Just a complete void. That's how I felt. Even with you on occasion. But that's not what I'm talking about. With Molly, I had actual excruciating physical pain in my heart. It felt like my heart was being squeezed until it would burst. I saw a cardiologist. I had EKGs and shit. The tests showed that my heart was actually enlarged. They put me on blood thinners like I was a goddamned senior citizen. At the age of nineteen! She did that to me. She disabled me. We said we'd always be there for each other, but she didn't keep her end of the deal. She was supposed to come back, but she didn't until a couple of months ago. And when she did, she brought that Adventure Ken doll dickwad with her. I had to sit there and smile every time she talked about how great he was. But it ripped into me. You know, I always said I just wanted her to be happy. Truth is, I wanted her to be miserable. I wanted the two of them to fail spectacularly. I wanted him to make her so, so unhappy. And then he did. Not in the way I expected. But, Emily, it's a chance for me. And if there's a chance, I gotta take it.

Information on this playwright may be found at www.alimaclean.com

SULLEN GIRL

Ali MacLean

BURT, a 40-year-old widower from Lehigh Valley, PA, has two speeds: volatile and drunk. Since losing his wife to cancer, his explosive temper has only intensified. BURT's ten-year-old daughter GEN wakes to find BURT, sitting on her bed. BURT, after stumbling home drunk from the local bar wants to talk to her. But then his abuse escalates to a new level.

BURT

Between you and your brother ... I'm just ... having a hard time with your mother not here. I'm trying, but I am having a hard time. I miss her. *(BURT grabs GEN in a bear hug and doesn't let go for a moment.)* I gotta do better. I just don't know what to do with the two of you now. I don't know how to do this alone. I feel like I got splinters in my brain. I fucking miss her. I hate that I have to be here without her. I'm not supposed to be without her. Some days I think they should've just buried me along with her. When I met her I had nothing. I didn't expect nothing. I didn't think someone like her would even look at me twice. I'd've done anything for her, she was so fucking beautiful. I even quit drinking for a while. Till Kellan came along. But yeah. She had some weird, mermaid power over me. Sometimes the only way I could get out from under her spell was to make her a little ugly for a few days. That's how beautiful she was to me ... *(He begins to cry.)* I still see her face when I shut my eyes. I go to sleep and I wanna keep sleeping because she's not dead when I'm sleeping. And when I wake up it hurts. It fucking hurts. *(Pause.)* And when I wake up I see you. You look more and more like her every day. You know what that does to me? Sometimes it's like seeing a ghost when you walk into the room, and for a moment I think I'm going berserk. You're her spitting image. You know that? You are getting to be so pretty, Genny. *(He strokes her hair. A pause.)* You're getting to be so grown up. *(He slides his hands under the covers.)* Now, be nice. *(A warning.)* Are you gonna be nice?

Information on this playwright may be found at
www.alimaclean.com

EIGHT NIGHTS

Jennifer Maisel

New York City. 1949. ERICH, 40s, German-Jewish, is seeing his daughter, Rebecca, 19, for the first time since she was 9. He had gone ahead to New York to set up a life for his family; after trying to get to the U.S. on the St. Louis, a ship that was turned back, she and her mother and sisters ended up in the camps where the others died. They are father and daughter and they are strangers.

ERICH

I didn't know they would send you back.

There was no good way about it — the deciding. We were up nights. Should I go? Should I not go? Should I take you or your sisters? But to take you away from your mother — you, who wouldn't go to sleep at night without her lying beside you. And then, when we heard about the St. Louis, the ship, it meant you were only a few months behind. We felt lucky.

It was agony. To be here. To not know.

Of course, it's nothing compared — I ... you will tell me.

Or you won't tell me.

I hated how much I was missing. The everyday of you showing me what you learned at school, of Nikki and her little laugh. Gerta and the way whenever she wasn't the center of attention she would throw herself down for a little bruise to get comfort and kisses.

But from the moment you set sail, May 13th, 1939, I felt less and less ... empty.

And then one night my friends who I stay with, they told me I had been screaming in my sleep. It had to have just been a bad dream, they said. But I knew.

And they turned the St. Louis — they turned you away from Cuba. They turned you away from this country, from Canada. They turned my hearts away and sent you back.

And when the letters stopped coming.

Rebecca, I would have given anything to be with you. I would have given anything —

Information on this playwright may be found at https://www.jennifermaisel.com/

ANTIGONE: 3021

Nina Mansfield

HAEMON, 15-19, a teenager in futuristic Thebes. HAEMON confronts his mother, the leader of Thebes, Chancellor Creah, because she plans to execute his girlfriend Antigone, and has also recently decided to execute Antigone's sister, Ismene.

HAEMON

When you don't have the support of the people, what kind of leader can you be? You say you want to hear what I have to say, but you don't. I question you — I question you for your own good, and it's like the tiniest hole poked in your massive ego reveals you're full of hot air. And when all that air seeps out, what are you left with? You can't rule without real substance. You can't rule with the force of your own ego. I'm not going to be one of those people who just says what you want to hear. Because you're wrong. Your law is wrong. The way you've handled this entire situation is wrong. You can't just kill people who disagree with you. And I'm not the only one who thinks so. Open your eyes, Mom. Look beyond *The Vista* and look into the actual streets of our city. I had faith in you once. But now, I'm going to do what I think is right. And don't worry. I'll never bother you again. Deactivate projection and log out.

Information on this playwright may be found at www.ninamansfield.com

THE HIGH GROUND

Jackie Martin

SIMON, he/his, a photojournalist in his late 20s to early 30s from a small town in Cape Cod, Massachusetts. SIMON is confessing to his mother why he avoided coming home for the holidays last year. In doing so, he is also admitting for the first time his complicated feelings toward his late brother and the family dynamic.

SIMON

Do you want to know why I didn't come home for Christmas last year? I was working. But only because I volunteered to work.

[HILLARY: In Uruguay.]

Talbot had been to visit me at the end of November. Do you remember? He took the bus to New York.

[HILLARY: I remember. He was excited. He'd never been.]

He was excited. I was … less so. *(Beat.)* I was angry. He'd already put you through so much in the last few years, and I was pissed that he wanted to spend money on a bus ticket rather than pay it back to you. But what was I supposed to do? My little brother wanted to visit me. See the city. Could I have said no? Knowing that he could go off the rails at any time and my last memory would be telling him I didn't want to see him? Getting him off the bus was horrible. I felt sick. I didn't know what to say. You know how people in movies check in with one another? Like, they really want to know how the other person is doing? That's not how I felt. That's not how we were. I asked Tal how he was doing, and I was terrified he'd tell me the truth — how hard he was battling. And then I'd have to have a conversation about that. And I'd have to decide what to do about it. But he said he was fine. After that, it got a little easier. It was like he was communicating some unspoken message — he understood the rules. We would have a lighthearted weekend, superficial conversation. And that's how it went. We had fun. We relaxed, I showed him around. I never asked one question about rehab, or therapy — not one time did I try to dig below the surface. I let myself pretend things were normal and that they were going to stay that way. But for us, that's not normal. What's normal for us is what happened two weeks later, when you called to tell me he'd gotten picked up again. He was using again. You were bailing him out. Again. And I hated him. And I hated myself for not checking in with him, not being a better brother. But I also couldn't bring myself to see him like that. I wasn't ready. I didn't want to see the shame in his eyes, and I didn't want him to see the rage in mine. I needed to spend my Christmas working, pretending Talbot was still the same easygoing, funny, sweet guy he'd been with me in New York. So. I'm sorry, but I also don't know if I regret it yet.

Information on this playwright may be found at
https://newplayexchange.org/users/29102/jackie-martin

WOLF AND BADGER

Michael John McGoldrick

LANDON, a 26-year-old drug dealer and brother to Maddox. He and another character have been scheming to undermine Maddox's confidence in himself. In the scene below, all three are playing cards while discussing the various men who had relationships with the boys' mother during their childhood.

LANDON

I did exaggerate. Because some of them stayed. And Martin was the worst. Trucker. Coke fiend. Badass. Used to get his buzz on and come looking for someone to hurt. Ain't that right, Maddox? *(Beat.)* And our sainted mother wouldn't do a damned thing about it. Now, Martin preferred Maddox cause he was smaller. Tiny, like a Badger. And when Martin came, Wolf would do what he could to protect the pack. Cause that's what a brother is for, yeah? So I'd force myself between them. End up taking a hit or two. Most times, that'd be enough. But this one time, I couldn't take it no more. So I found it. The courage. To stand. Cold-cocked Martin in the face. And he thrashed me within an inch of my life. In the hospital for two weeks. I nearly died. But that's what it took to get Ma to kick him out of the house. *(Beat.)* Sorry. Is it my play? *(Beat.)* I learned something from that. You ain't a man until you learn to stand against anybody — anybody — who's gonna tear you down. Something my little brother has never learned in the whole of his pussy life. *(He plays a card.)* Goddammit, I love cards.

Information on this playwright may be found at
https://newplayexchange.org/users/5535/michael-john-mcgoldrick

HITCH

James McLindon

LANE, thirties, a FedEx driver on vacation, a bit dorky, but in a good mood and rather full of himself at the moment. LANE is mansplaining hitchhikers to his passenger, an 18ish-looking hitchhiker he has just picked up, trying to draw her into a conversation.

LANE

Hardly anybody picks up hitchhikers anymore. Everyone thinks it's way too dangerous these days, I guess. Don't get me wrong, you gotta be careful who you pick up or what car you get into and all that. And even then, not everybody is what they seem at first. But it's probably no more dangerous now than it ever was. I mean, people are basically good. That doesn't change. People stay the same. It's just like, I don't know, like ... child molesters. *(LANE smiles at the young woman, who apparently has become a little concerned at the mention of child molesting.)* No, no, I just mean, we're more aware of it now. Take autism, that's a better example. Newspapers, cable news, talk radio, they all do stories on autism, right, and we get more aware of it, and being more aware just makes it seem like there's more of it. But really, there isn't. Cuz people are people are people and they don't change. *(LANE turns to look at her.)* What, you don't have any opinion? *(LANE waits for a response. None is forthcoming.)* Oh, yeah, I see your point. You totally persuaded me. You're not super friendly, are you? I could've just driven past you back there, y'know. The least you could do is talk a little since I'm giving you a ride.

Information on this playwright may be found at http://www.jamesmclindon.com

WHEN MARSHMALLOWS BURN

Tara Meddaugh

SAMMY, 8-12 years old, but designed to be played by a teen or young adult. While roasting marshmallows by the fire, SAMMY has started to transform into a werewolf for the very first time, which frightens his mother. SAMMY doesn't want to trouble his mother for the raw meat he now craves, so he runs to the woods to catch a squirrel himself. He returns to his mother after devouring his first kill in the hopes of making her proud.

SAMMY

(to his mother) I ran in the woods, then crouched down and was really quiet. After just a couple of seconds, I saw a squirrel — because, Mom, now I can see in the dark better than normal! So then, I jumped up, super-fast, and ran to the squirrel, super super-fast! And I put my mouth on the squirrel's body and chomped down and just started chewing! The fur and bones didn't even bother me! I guess that's what my fangs are for. I think I ate most of it in like, 5 bites. That's good, right? I always thought I was slower than most kids, but now, I might be faster than anyone! *(pause)* Mom? *(pause)* You're proud of me, right? *(pause)* Do you want me to get you a squirrel now? *(pause)* You can burn it in the fire if you don't want to eat it raw. I know you're not like me. *(pause)* I know I'm not like you anymore. *(pause)* Are you mad at me? *(pause)* Mom? Are you gonna talk to me again? *(pause)* Did you only love me because I was a human kid?

Information on this playwright may be found at https://www.tarameddaugh.com/

THE GREAT LATKE SHOWDOWN OF 20 AUGHT 9

D. Lee Miller

MATTHEW, Father, 40s or older. MATTHEW must disappoint his son, JUSTIN, 10, when he explains why the family can't use the beautiful menorah JUSTIN made for Chanukah. They go to the park to talk, man-to-man. The father devises a partly true story of a similar menorah to spare his son's feelings.

MATTHEW

We played more dreidel. Sang more songs and in a few minutes the latkes were done. We would eat soon. We gathered around the menorah in the kitchen, said the blessings and lit the candles. Then we all went into the dining room so the women could cool off for a moment. Suddenly, there was a POP! Zing! Gunshot sounds like the OK Corral. Your mother called 911; your grandma pushed her emergency alert because she thought she was having a heart attack. Alan and I ran into the kitchen using cookbooks as shields — only to see your sister's menorah shooting off tiles and nuts every which way. The candles themselves went flying — one hit the drapes which caught on fire which ignited the dried flowers on the windowsill and sparked the table's centerpiece. Alan and I threw soup bowls of water wherever was needed. A couple of candles fell into Aunt Marci's latkes and they started to burn, so I threw water on them, too. When the firemen came and hosed the kitchen, the lights shorted and we went into darkness. That's when your mother yelled. After the commotion, we sat down in the living room with some flashlights. Unofficially, your mother won the latke showdown because hers were protected by the warm oven which luckily saved the brisket, too. The miracle of that Chanukah was that our house didn't burn down. That and Uncle Alan was only in the hospital overnight after he slipped on the kitchen floor.

That and the fire department said Aunt Marci's latkes should have only burned for a few minutes but they burned all night.

Information on this playwright may be found at
https://newplayexchange.org/users/36442/d-lee-miller

AMPHITRITE AND POSEIDON: A MEMORY OF WATER

John Minigan

POSEIDON, the God of the Sea, has been searching for Amphitrite, a water nymph and potential bride, but she's been hiding from him. Trident in hand, he tries to bring the audience to see things from his point-of-view.

POSEIDON

Amphitrite! I coulda sworn she came in here.

(He addresses the audience.)

Oh, hey there. I'm sure you recognize me. Don't you?

Poseidon. I know, I know. The Trident. Gives it away, right?

It's so I can control the sea.

My father, Kronos, he got things divvied up:

Hades got the Underworld. Zeus got the Sky. I got the Sea.

"Hey, Dad," I said. "I can't swim."

He said, *"Learn."*

And, you know, he ate most of my brothers and sisters, so I said, "All right, Dad!"

"You must control the sea," he said.

I said, "Hey, Dad. All I got's a Trident. How's that supposed to control the sea? It's like eating soup with a fork."

He had no answer for that.

But, like I said, he ate most of my brothers and sisters, so I figure, work with what you got.

Amphitrite! Where are you?

I saw her dancing, her and her sisters. She's got maybe fifty of them. *Big* family.

But *her*. She's a looker, I'll tell you that. See her once, you're not gonna forget!

And what's it look like: Poseidon, mighty God of the Sea, still *single*?

Amphitrite! Where is —

Oh, look. You're right there, behind all these people. Come on out, babe!

I want to marry you!

Information on this playwright may be found at http://www.johnminigan.com/

SHERIDAN

Christian Missonak

ETHAN, a 30-something working stiff from Chicago, is venting to his brother MARK at a local tiki bar after getting into an argument with his girlfriend and actress, LUCY. ETHAN and LUCY have been struggling in the aftermath of a stillbirth.

ETHAN

I don't know what to do anymore. I really don't. I don't know if anybody can help her and clearly I can't and I'm — I'm sick of trying. She's not going to the therapist. I think she's just content to wallow in this forever. And it's not like she needs to be over it. I'm not over it but at a certain point I would think — you know what really pisses me off? I don't even know how much of this is real. You know? I mean, it's Lucy. Is she actually this upset or has she just played fucking … I don't know … Ophelia so many times she thinks this is what grief is supposed to look like. She's always got to be the star of the show, even in this. Everyone's got to know that her grief is the most interesting and complex of all possible griefs. And apparently that just gives her carte blanche to say whatever the fuck she wants. Before you got here, like literally right before, you know what she told me? She said that I thought the baby was disgusting after it was born. Apparently, I hadn't taken a picture. Lucy came out of it and she wanted to see a picture and I … I didn't have one. But it wasn't that I thought the baby was … everything was happening so quickly — it didn't occur to me to pull out my phone in that exact moment … I still thought there'd be other, you know, better opportunities but it wasn't … and no. OK? No. I didn't like the way she looked. She looked like a baby that wasn't going to make it. And that wasn't necessarily something I wanted to remember. But I didn't think she looked disgusting. I never would have thought that. There's no way that I thought that.

Information on this playwright may be found at
https://www.christianmissonak.com

BIG BEN AND THE JUICE FAST

Pamela Morgan

BIG BEN, a cockroach who has been living for years with Meg, a habitual dieter. They are hungry and have finally had enough of Meg's current diet trend: the juice fast.

BIG BEN

What do I want?

It isn't what I want, Meg. It's what I need!

What WE need.

Food! We need food, Meg!

You've been starving us for months.

First with Weight Watchers and counting those damn points.

Seriously, I know they say eggs don't count, but not when you eat a dozen a day.

If I never see a hard-boiled egg again, I would die a happy cockroach.

After that, we tried, what was it? The keto diet?

Don't get me wrong. I will bathe myself in meat and cheese any time you want.

But no carbs ever?

That's not healthy for us, Meg.

Now it's juice fasting.

Juice fasting? That isn't a thing!

It's either fasting or it's juice.

I'm drawing the line. I've had enough.

Or, in this case, not enough!

It is time we made a change.

I have to maintain this figure, Meg, you think I can do that on juice?

And my children! All two thousand, seven hundred and eleven of them.

I can't come home every morning with fruit pulp and juiced kale.

Don't we deserve better than this, Meg?

Look at us.

Up in the middle of the night, raiding the kitchen for random scraps of food.

Is this who we are?

Is this what we've become?

I'm hungry, Meg.

I mean, really hungry.

The soul-crushing kind of hungry.

And I'm a cockroach; I can live for a month without food.

Heck, I can live a week without my head.

But can you, Meg? Can you?

Isn't it time we ate?

Information on this playwright may be found at
https://pamelamorganwrites.com

SIDEBURNS

Rich Orloff

MAN, who can be played either by an older man recalling the described experience, or a teenager going through the experience. As he shaves, the MAN looks at himself in the mirror and relives being a teenaged usher at the 1968 Democratic Convention in Chicago.

MAN

I've just gotten a job as one of hundreds of ushers at the 1968 Democratic National Convention in my hometown, Chicago. I'm way too young for the job — you're supposed to be eighteen and I'm nowhere close — but my dad has connections with the company providing the ushers, and so I get the job. I'm still too young to realize that *this* is how Chicago works.

On Wednesday, on the podium, a senator from Connecticut denounces the Chicago police's response to demonstrators in Grant Park as "Gestapo tactics". I can see Mayor Daley on the convention floor. His beet-red face is spewing invectives I can't hear but I can imagine. Suddenly it feels like everyone is yelling and cursing. It is the greatest congregation of anger I have seen in my life.

Thursday, before the final session of the convention begins, the ushers are told there's gonna be a change. Mayor Daley is going to have some "guests" attend today. Although none of them will have the proper pass, they must get top priority in seating.

Hundreds of Daley supporters have been bussed in to the convention, and it feels like most of them have been herded into my section. They've been given take-out chicken dinners and large signs which say: "WE LOVE MAYOR DALEY!" There aren't enough seats for them, but I'm told to let them sit in the aisles, stand in the back, or anywhere they can squeeze. Every inch of my section is packed, even though the other spectators, the ones with the proper passes, they haven't even arrived yet.

When they do, well, it's obvious to anyone that there is *no* room. But people still argue and beg to be let in. A quiet little man in a loud sports jacket pleads with me to let him in. He looks as if he's pleaded with every other usher and I am his last hope. He has the proper pass, but what can I do?

On the podium, a speaker begins to denounce Daley and what's called a police riot against protesters. Immediately, as if on cue, everyone in my section raises their signs and starts to chant, "WE LOVE DALEY! WE LOVE DALEY!" And they keep chanting till the speaker leaves the stage.

For the first time in my short life, I realize that the people in power have no more respect for the rules than the people demonstrating against them. They'll follow the rules when they are served by them but will ignore them the moment the rules get in their way.

I feel ... betrayed.

I let the pleading man in. I let in anyone who can squeeze in. The "guests" of Daley complain about the crowding but ... but I no longer care.

I will listen to my own rules now, not theirs.

Information on this playwright may be found at
https://www.richorloff.com/

DIAMOND WOMAN

Nicholas Priore

MARK, a body-builder in his early 20s, sits at his dying mother's bedside in the nursing home where she once worked. Her last visitors have left and she has fallen asleep, giving him a chance to say what he has to say ...

MARK

Tell 'em how you scraped and suffered and sacrificed at the expense of joy and decency and basic human dignity all for your savior, say you wanna see him so you can tell him yourself about how you worked all those double shifts changin' piss'n shit fuckin sheets and bedpans feedin' your four big dumb wop sons for all these years while caring for an invalid husband with a dent in his head almost as bad as the truck he totaled, no help from his big Italian family, that you were given children who were physically and mentally beyond your control, and yet you hold it all together, put yourself on display, let 'em exploit our situation for that fuckin beyond scared straight show just so David could end up worse than before and then all the more ridiculed for it and not just him, but you too, people are so fuckin cruel, don't even know us, see a little kid and his mother all pathetic on TV and somehow come to blame you for a six two three hundred pound teenager fuckin' up, and now, no matter how big or strong I get, I'll always be that little shit on TV cryin' how he's afraid of his big brother, and no matter how much I try to help David, he will always be the scumbag from when that show came to OCJ, all that embarrassment, all meant to help us, and for what, it wasn't bad enough, all we had goin' on, now everyone has to know about it? Disgracing the legacy of the strongest and most special person ever to leave this earth? Yea. You tell 'em about all that, how you were the real savior and no one came to your rescue. Whatever they got goin' on up there, do not let 'em fuck with you like at the social security office, whatever it is, you deserve your reward. And lemme tell ya what else, this better not be it. A bed to die in at the Masonic Home? After working here all your life, you clean the soiled linen of other people's death bed sheets, just so you could lie in 'em yourself? Is this really the fuckin' bed you've made? Then again, you are in your glory, aren't ya? They treat you like a queen here, got you in the biggest room they got, big TV for your stories. I bet you appreciate the hell outta that, ha, makin' all these beds all these years, now you finally get to lay down, let em wait on you for once … makin' the best of it as always, while you wait on God — Oh, and I'm sure, in all your pain, you still wanna stick around about as much as we all want you to, but don'chu worry about it, you do what you gotta do, okay? You hear me? I'll figure my shit out, you know it, and David too. As for Dad, still no clue how he outlives you but I'll look after him as best I can since Matt and Vinnie won't have it, and they can take care'a themselves from now on. You were always our rock down here, but now, you're more than that. Under the crushing pressure of it all, you found your true form … and you're a diamond. Not just beautiful or indestructible, but that shine, I don't need to see it, I can feel that warm glow from anywhere, even after you're gone … even when mine is runnin' low … and I'll follow that to wherever you are … or nowhere, I don't care, I'm goin there. Oh, but in the meantime, don't do what people always ask the dead to do and watch over us, fuck that shit, you did that all along, you got better shit ahead'a ya now … I hope … and I'm not so sure I want you seein' what I'm doin' day to day anyway, it was bad enough in life … no I'm only teasin', you know what I mean though, just go and don't look back. Okay, I can see you're tired, so I'll let you … I'll let you go … hope to see you when you wake up … or whenever … not sure whether to tell you about your granddaughter or not, I want you to know, but I don't want you leavin' with any regret, you seem so at peace with it and I'm not sure you'll … I don't know if she'll get here in time. Either way, I got this … and you got this, so no lingering, when the time comes to get goin, I want you to fly on outta here … you hear me? And if you … when you get to Heaven, don't forget to tell em what I said …

Information on this playwright may be found at
https://nextstagepress.com/teenie/

CLIMBING THE GOOD WALLS

Robin Rice

LOU is a lonely guy . His job working for the city parks service disappeared with the outbreak of a virus that ravaged the world. LOU has been more alone than ever for a long time, but now, with the virus in retreat, he confronts it with newfound strength.

LOU

Hey, get back here! Like it or not, it happened. A shift away from selfish has happened.

Before we enjoyed what people did for us but didn't really pay attention to anyone except families and close friends. Before, we used people — to run trains, sell food, sell clothes; used them to build buildings and bridges, entertain us, write books, raise crops, teach, heal, make, clean. We went on marches, wrote letters, worried about oppressed people. Some did; some didn't or didn't so much. It was stop and start. Peripheral to our lives. We would have gone on the same but you pushed us smack up against a wall and shut us up.

Shut apart, away from the rat race, day-to-day thoughts didn't apply anymore. We started to think like Magellan, Hillary, Heyerdahl …

We began thinking about who we are when we're alone; who we are together; what "together" means. Thank you for that. Not for those who died or suffered and still suffer but thank you on behalf of those who made it through.

We changed. We are changed.

Back when it looked like New York would go under, 30,000 nurses and doctors from other states came to help us. Volunteers. Yes, volunteers. Why do you think they came?

Then we helped other states. And other states helped other states. *Why?* Don't cover your ears. You're going to hear this and hear good. It's the truth. Facts. Reality. We've learned a lot. You may still lurk in corners, but against all of us together, in the future you don't stand a chance in hell.

Information on this playwright may be found at
www.RobinRicePlaywright.com

CAPRICCIO RADIO

Larry Rinkel

JAMES GODFREY, late 20s, recently promoted as director of a media conglomerate of which the Capriccio network is a part, is reviewing the performance of all announcers on staff and giving a dressing-down to the snobbish and pompous CLAUDE FEIERSTEIN.

GODFREY

Same hoity-toity our-shit-don't-stink attitude I get from all you classical types. Look, Claude. I've got eight radio stations. I can't have one set of announcers thinking only their music is the best and all the others suck. 'Cause there's people out there, Claude, they love their music maybe more than life itself, maybe even more than you love yours.

I'm going to tell you a story. Before I came here, I spent four years managing Carlos Suarez, in my opinion the greatest country singer of his time. Ever hear of him?

No, I didn't think so. Well, we were touring all these little towns, 'cause Carlos wanted everyone should have a chance to hear him. So one morning we pull into this Alabama truck stop, and this skinny kid behind the counter, 18, 19, scraggly little beard, well he sees Carlos and he goes, "Hey, man, I'm comin' to your concert tonight." So Carlos goes, "Cool, where ya sittin'?" and the kid points way up, you know the cheap seats, and Carlos he puts on this wicked grin and says, "Oh no you're not," and he comps the kid four house seats fifth row center, backstage passes, steak dinner on us, and you wouldn't believe this kid's face.

So the kid brings his friend, their girlfriends, Carlos dedicates sets to the girlfriends, and afterwards we give them gift bags — posters, photos, all his CDs, hand-signed, the works. And just that morning here was this nobody behind a counter frying bacon and eggs, but that night he cleaned up, nice threads, boots, a little style, and the kid, he kept shaking Carlos's hand and saying over and over, "Best day of my life, man, best fuckin' day of my life."

And I only saw it then, the kid had these beautiful ice-blue eyes, glowing like sapphires, and Carlos he says to me, "Four little angels, Jim. I just saw four little angels come down from heaven." And are you going to tell me what that kid and his friends went through doesn't matter because it's not your artsy-fartsy highfalutin classical music? You understand me, Claude? Anything you want to say?

Information on this playwright may be found at
https://newplayexchange.org/users/7668/larry-rinkel

CAPRICCIO RADIO

Larry Rinkel

NOAH BROCK, age 17, is a budding composer who has heard a rumor that his favorite classical station, the Capriccio network, is likely shutting down. NOAH visits the station and gets into a discussion about his own ambitions as a composer.

NOAH

There was one good teacher at my school, the theory teacher Mr. Fiske. He doesn't understand my music, but he told me about this young composers contest, which I entered and I won fourth place, Most Promising. So I thought maybe four people entered, but I asked and it was 178!

What, you think my parents were proud? I didn't even tell my parents. My parents think I'm this ugly skinny freak who dyes his hair and writes this weird music nobody understands. It's like my mom's always going, "Why don't you have a game of one-on-one with Brandon. That's why we put up that net." Well, screw you, Mom. Why don't any of you listen to my music? And then my dad gets all mad when I don't join in their stupid sports talk at dinner. Like I'm supposed to be Superjock Brandon who's all about who won the game and what Coach said about his swing and let's watch some moron getting himself killed doing 200 miles an hour on NASCAR! Don't they understand, if I'm not saying anything it's 'cause I've got this whole world racing around my head and I've got to write down what I'm hearing after dessert. And they'll never know because they don't give a crap about me. I hate my family. I hate my brother, I hate adults. OK, most adults. Not you.

Information on this playwright may be found at https://newplayexchange.org/users/7668/larry-rinkel

THE AGENCY

Laura Rohrman

KEVIN, 57, a worn-out literary agent has just returned to the office from his brother's funeral. In this monologue, he's grieving and realizing life is short and that his best days are likely behind him.

KEVIN

He's my brother. My only brother. He was better at basketball than me. He could shoot a basket from 25 feet away. He was only 60. Life goes so fast, you know. His heart. The thing is … my parents are gone now, and he's gone. It's just me. And I'm 57. And 10 years ago, I was 47 … and before that … 15 years ago I sold a book about the greatest basketball players of all time. Did you know that? There were 20 publishers bidding for it. Two hundred and fifty thousand. And I got the commission. Did you know that? After that everyone wanted me as their agent — all the great athletes. That swimmer guy — I brought that one in. I'm the guy. I could easily make a basket from 15 feet away. But I've got this thing now. My heart beats too fast sometimes. When Anne comes back can you tell her I brought her these flowers? They're from the funeral. It's not like I bought them special or anything. But I wanted her to know that I liked her performance. She was too young of course … but she knocked it out of the park … or theater or whatever. The critics may have ripped her apart, but there was something about it. Her cadence. Or maybe it was just that I know her … or … it was her voice, the tremor, the calm, the *(he thinks, breaks away)*. She reminded me of my mom. I kept seeing my mom up there. My mom would spank us for staying outside and getting all dirty. "Come inside right now young man." But even when she screamed, and her eyes would be popping out of her head with rage … she always wanted to be an actress. She was in the school plays and then when we were older; she settled for acting in local plays. She even had a little school. We always felt like she was mad

at us, like she didn't really want us. It wasn't that. She was just …
so pretty … and her voice … it was like she was always singing.

He pauses and looks up.

Information on this playwright may be found at
https://newplayexchange.org/users/1786/laura-rohrman

RUSSIAN TROLL

Rich Rubin

ALEXEI, mid-thirties, is a Russian intelligence officer working at the Internet Research Agency, a Kremlin-sponsored, top-secret organization whose mission is to destabilize the West using various modes of cyber-warfare. He addresses the twenty or so (unseen) operatives under his supervision.

ALEXEI

All right, you fuckers!

Listen up!

It's now September 19th, and do any of you geniuses know why that's important?

(Beat.)

No?

Alright, then let me tell you:

That means we have exactly fifty days — a little over seven weeks — until the presidential election.

Not ours, of course.

The one in America.

So who will it be, ladies and gentlemen, boys and girls?

Candidate "A," who slapped us with sanctions after Crimea?

Or Candidate "B," who brought Miss Universe to Moscow and named his favorite daughter "Ivanka" in honor of one of Russia's most celebrated monarchs, Ivan the Terrible?

Yes, yes, I know:

It's actually a bit more complicated than that.

But for now, let's just keep it simple, shall we?

Don't forget the basics:

Candidate "B":

Good.

Candidate "A":

Bad.

Just keep that in mind, and everything else will follow.

Oh.

And one other thing to keep in mind, a reminder of why all of us are here:

"You fuck with Mother Russia, you're bound to lose your cock — and even if you're a lady, don't think this doesn't apply to you!"

(Beat.)

I have no idea what that last part means, but it's an old Russian saying.

Well … at least according to my Grandma, my *babushka*, it's an old Russian saying.

And believe me if anyone's an old Russian, *she* is!

Information on this playwright may be found at
www.richrubinplaywright.com

MY STRUGGLE

Cindi Sansone-Braff

*Set in 1981, the Sunnydale Nursing Home staff celebrates the
100th birthday of their oldest resident, DR. ABRAHAM KASPER.
DR. KASPER, a holocaust survivor, takes a disturbing trip down
memory lane as he laments the dire consequences of not listening to
divine guidance.*

DR. KASPER

Ah, it is you, Magdalena. The best birthday gift of all. My favorite
aide! Such a pretty, Polish girl, who does not speak a word of
English but smiles so gently at me and never complains. How
tragic to think that she must spend her youth changing this *alte
kaker's* dirty diapers and bearing witness to a wrinkled 100-year-
old *touchas*. Life can be so cruel sometimes. Oh, Magdalena, you
should be out dancing, romancing, making love, making babies,
making mischief, not locked away among the dead and dying. *(As
MAGDALENA is changing his diaper, he lets out a fart.)* Oh, excuse
me! So sorry. *(MAGDALENA lets out a giggle.)* Glad you find this
amusing! Here I am worrying that I am going to gas this poor
Polish girl to death as she wipes down my bottom, and she laughs.
Farts and giggles! The universal language. So, my dear, everyone
kept asking me today, "Dr. Kasper, how did you get to live to be
100?" "Eat lots of onions and garlic!" Always the jokester! That
is me! Why tell the truth? There is nothing worse in this world
than to have to listen to the kvetching of an old *mashugana* who
has lost his faith. And so, I smile and laugh, and dole out bits of
wisdom, offer words of praise and encouragement. Why I even
willingly partake in whatever lame entertainment the "Rah-rah, sis
boom bah!" recreation director has concocted for the amusement
of the residence, whether it be the boredom of Bingo Night or the
banality of the brain games. I am, however, always careful to give
the illusion that I am a team player, a pious and righteous man.

"Dr. Kasper is a living saint," they say. "He's always upbeat and fun!" "Dr. Kasper always has a smile on his face!" Illusion. Life is so much grandstanding, pretension, peacocking, propaganda, if you will. "The Big Lie," we tell because the truth is too brutal to bear. And besides, who would believe the truth if I told them? But Magdalena, since you must suffer the indignity of giving this decrepit body a sponge bath, and since you cannot understand more than a few words of English, this will not interfere with my vow to take my deep, dark secret of longevity to the grave. Just between you and me, sadly, no one else, who knew this secret, ever lived to tell. So, on this snowy March night, on the 100-year celebration of my life, I will tell you the tale of how Abraham Kasper, a family physician from Vienna, came to live to be the oldest resident in the Sunnydale Nursing Home. One hundred years … that is an obscenely long time to live, now, isn't it?

Information on this playwright may be found at
https://newplayexchange.org/users/45654/cindi-sansone-braff

GETTING LUCKY

Chris Shaw Swanson

With the kids overnight at grandma's, JOHN is eager and poised to "get lucky" with his wife when he discovers his young daughter's beloved hamster Max dead in its cage. Not wanting his evening derailed, JOHN endeavors to revive (CPR) and hide the hamster from his wife until he's overcome with guilt.

JOHN

Max. He's ... he's dead. When I went to feed him, I found him kaput in his cage. I was selfish, I didn't want to ruin our evening, so I ... I stuck him in the ice bucket — yes — that was cold of me — but he was dead and I was horny-in-lust-with-you and nothing I could do at that moment was going to change his being dead or my being horny. I'm scum, Barb. Because I lied and that is hugely wrong. I want to be that great man our kids can look up to ... and I hate falling short. But when I ... when I desire you, I'm willing to cheat, lie, steal, touch dead rodents with my bare *(touches lips)* ... hands ... because that feeling for you makes me forget about everything else. Even sanitation. I'm not some rock. I'm not him. Or it. I'm just a guy who is crazy about his wife.

Information on this playwright may be found at https://www.chrisshawswanson.com/

THE KNOWN UNIVERSE

Scott C. Sickles

THE KNOWN UNIVERSE *is the final play in* THE SECOND WORLD TRILOGY, *a love story between two men from when they're 11-years-old until the end of the world nearly 50 years later.*

2067. The Earth is entering a new ice age and nothing on the surface will survive. Astronaut Anzor is in a space station, in orbit, facilitating evacuation efforts. His family has been waiting on Earth to be rescued. Anzor has just informed them — his husband, TEDDY; their two young sons; and the boys' mother and stepmother — that further evacuation efforts have been abandoned, and they have less than two hours left before the planet becomes uninhabitable. Anzor and his family bid each other a long farewell. In this scene, TEDDY — a 58-year-old Korean American scientist — takes a moment alone on the video call with Anzor, who has just expressed concern that TEDDY is being too calm about the bad news.

[Note: Dialogue in brackets is for context only and should not be spoken. Also, this is a rant! Do not add unscripted pauses. If it takes longer than three minutes, you're too slow.]

TEDDY

Of course I'm being rational about this. What choice do I have?! We have less than two hours to live. I can't waste time on bullshit and hysterics! Once the kids close their eyes and ... [go to sleep for the last time] *That* is when I will lose my shit. Not a second ... [before]

(Pause.)

That said ... I just can't believe I'm never going to touch you again. *That* is my problem. There's all this space, this distance, and I need you here to hold my atoms together. But instead, I have to do that myself and I hate it. I have fucking loved you since we were eleven years old! Before I even knew what you looked like! I fell in love with your name and your words and your cursive, and I deserve better than this! I deserve to die in your goddamn arms! I deserve to feel the last warmth and heat I ever feel coming from your body. *We* deserve fucking better!

All I have right now are two kids who were supposed to have a much, much, much longer life. Instead, they get this. The last thing that will ever happen to them is a shitty nap in a hotel room. They don't get to die in your arms either! Which, of course, is better for you. You won't see any of this. You won't feel that heat leave our bodies. And you will live.

Don't get me wrong, I want to live too! I want to live on, and on and on and on, all of us beside you, worrying about low-gravity bone density and staving off boredom.

My god, our kids are magnificent! They are smart and nasty and just the best little bastards ever. Given time, our children could have saved the damn world. But that's not gonna happen, so here we are! And there you are. There … you … are!

(Pause.)

Anyway, what I'm trying to say is when the rest of us down here are gone, our problems are over! And yes, it's gonna suck to be you. You won't have us. Sure, hearts, mind, memory. But all of that will fade; there's no stopping it. It will just happen. And this already unbearable distance will only get greater and greater until even the planet we're standing on is a memory. All that will be left of our magnificence will be in your head. And you will miss it and grieve for it, but it will live on there! And it will inspire you to live a great life far away.

(Pause.)

I need a hug.

Information on this playwright may be found at
https://newplayexchange.org/users/2036/scott-sickles

EX-GAY BAR

David Simpatico

COSMO, a recent ex-gay convert in his early 30s, confesses he still believes two men can fall in love. But why does it have to be so hard?

COSMO

No, love *is* possible. I just never met the right man. Because I confused lust for love. I had this desperate need to be desired, fucking three, four guys a night, the more guys wanted me the more I was loved, right? But they didn't want *me*, they wanted my body, my mouth, my ass, my cock, like I was a collection of body parts that didn't add up to anything —

The loneliness was unbearable. I just wanted to be loved. But on those rare occasions when a totally nice guy would express more than a fleeting interest in me, I'd boot him out, swipe left, delete, next, like a gerbil wheel of sex and shame. I didn't even hesitate, I figured rejection was just part of the gay lifestyle.

Two years ago, New Year's Eve, I'm sitting in the corner of a packed gay bar. The lone papi chulo, again. All that manic happiness, the whole desperate gay swirl of colognes and armpits. And I'm sitting alone, at two minutes to midnight, crying in the corner, looking for someone, anyone, on Grinder, Scruff, Daddyhunt — And this older guy, maybe 50, but sexy, he stands near me in the corner, grabs me right at midnight, kisses me, deep. Amazing. I'm stunned. He chose me. He's kissing me. He wraps me up like he's been waiting for me my entire life. Then, he turns to this other guy who's been watching us make out, he leans across me, says to the guy, *about* me, "Yeah, I know, I can do better." The other guy looks at me like, are you going to take that shit? And I do, I take it.

Because I agree with him. He can do better. I can barely keep from sobbing. I wrap my scarf around my face, head home in a blizzard. Tears freeze my eyelashes shut. *(Fighting sudden tears)* Why is it easier to suck someone's cock than it is to just be yourself?

Information on this playwright may be found at
https://newplayexchange.org/users/6145/david-simpatico

THE DEVIL SMOKES AMERICAN SPIRITS: A PLAY IN TEN CIGARETTES

Melissa Toomey

JOSIAH, 20s-30s, the dangerous and charismatic leader of a mysterious desert cult known as the People of Zion. Here, he corners his wife, MARY, in a gas station convenience store after she attempts to flee the cult for good.

JOSIAH

MARY? *(He pounds on the door)* Hey. Come outta there. HEY! It's not *anger. Anger* has no place, I told you. You don't seem to understand the nature of what it is you've done. You know this, it's in the Bible. It's in our hearts. Our people are in jeopardy. There are consequences. YOU CAN'T LEAVE ME OTHERWISE I AM POISONED FOREVER HAVING MET YOU. We have oaths to fulfill. The prophecy. The Love. That's what's real. That's what exists. That's what truth is. What you believe in doesn't matter because the truth doesn't require belief. *Love* is true. The future needs you. You feel it. Don't you?

Fine.

Go do what you want, Mary, but I know that you don't know what that is. Go ahead. Go wander around in the desert. Once you're out in that wide world of Babylon and you realize you're completely alone, you'll remember why you came home. You'll come back begging.

You know there's something out there we dreamed of escaping that we can't talk about because there aren't words for it. You've felt it and you feel it. It's that empty evil crammed in between a whole lot of normal little things. You can't escape it out here. No one's gonna understand. You're never gonna find a different truth than the one right here. You know who you are.

Zion is home. Home isn't what you want, it's where you're wanted. Where you're needed. Where you stop feeling afraid. You're never gonna find the Love we have for you because it's a kind we built. Your people need you. You have a responsibility as The Mother.

I … I need you too … You think about whether or not you wanna understand me. *(pause)*

Get some unfluoridated water while you're in here.

I'll wait for you outside.

Information on this playwright may be found at
www.melissatoomey.com

STONES THROW

Michael Towers

OLDER GENTLEMEN is a life-long resident of a small town that has endured changes at the hands of developers who seek to profit from a recent housing boom. After his new neighbor ignores the clearly marked property lines in an effort to improve the curb appeal of both houses, the OLDER GENTLEMEN confronts the 'blow in' with a lesson on community, connection and legacy.

OLDER GENTLEMAN

You wanna buy my house?

And tear it to the ground like the one you tore down to build that mini mansion?

My grandfather built that house with his bare hands and it stood there for a hundred years. Along with that flag pole. Your "guys" and your machine took'em both down in less than a day.

Round here we build things that last. Things that stand for something. Things with *roots*! Things that connect us to place long after we're gone.

People like you always talk in terms of numbers. You put money before things that matter. You may have a lot of it but not one penny of it cares about you back. Not like the Kane's across the street. Father built a house on either side for his son and daughter and they live there today. Or the Waterhouses next to 'em. Or the Fitzgeralds down the block! I'm gonna die in this house and if I'm lucky they'll bury me right over there where I put the dogs down before me.

So, you go on and make your fun. Flip your house — make your money and move on to the next one. But don't expect they'll build you a monument over on Thomas Drive or anywhere else for that matter. Then again, maybe if they do, some big shot from out of town will come along someday and tear it down.

Just to make a buck. Because that's what they do.

Information on this playwright may be found at
https://newplayexchange.org/users/68449/michael-towers

THE BIG RED NAUGAHYDE BOOTH (OR, WOULD-BE ELKS)

Jennie Webb

ZACH, a youthful-looking man who is probably in his early 30s, has spent an extraordinary evening with his older girlfriend and her friends, having dropped in to their regular girls-night-out. He shares this out-of-time story of his experience after leaving the bar with the audience while observing the women onstage.

ZACH

When I was little I had a teacher who always said to me, "Nothing ever turns out like you think it will." Like that's a bad thing.

So … I met this woman, this friend of my mother's. And it was cool because immediately I really liked her. It was all incredibly easy. It's not usually that way with me. And we get ready to listen to this tape — which she has never heard, never listened to all these years because it was mine — but before we turned it on she asked if I wanted to listen to it alone … Only it seemed right that she be there, because I could see how much she loved my mother. I mean, loved her. Really, really loved her.

At the start of the tape, I'm like, wow. I mean I've heard my mother's voice before in videos but this is different because this time it's for *me*. And as the voice goes on this friend goes totally berserk, she's crying and I'm crying and she — my mother — is talking about the weather and her parents and my bathroom habits at three and her medical reports and hospitals and how much everything was costing and my dad's being angry and her being angry and did I, at three, know they were angry and how was that affecting the weather and her parents and my bathroom habits …

Well. It became very clear that the voice on the tape wasn't my mother. I mean, not really. By the time she made this tape my mother was already ... very sick.

So I get this and I'm disappointed and the tape is still playing, but I look over at this woman, this friend, and she's stopped crying. She looks horrified. She looks panicked. She looks me in the eye and I can tell that she thinks ... she's failed.

My god, I've never felt so awful for anyone in my life. I go to hold her and say, "It's okay! It's okay! It's okay!" and for the first time ever I hear in my voice, my mother's voice. And I believe myself: that it is okay.

Then this woman — who by this time is bawling again like a maniac; we both are — says to me, "I'm so sorry!" And I'm ready to do my magical "it's okay" again so that I can be the one to make everything better ... Only she stops me.

With, "Well ... I guess the truth is, if you want to know your mother, you'll have to meet her friends."

Information on this playwright may be found at
www.jenniewebbsite.com

THE GUY WHO JUMPED INTO THE ZOO

Chris Widney

THE GUY, 25, fit, handsome. Although he's from upstate, THE GUY'S roots are in the city and he talks and sounds more like a "New Yawker." THE GUY is in a police interrogation room in The Bronx. He is nervous, jittery, suspicious.

THE GUY

That day? You wanna know about that day?

… I'm on the monorail ride. My car's empty. In the next one over is this pasty white family. Fat, snotty kid — tossing "Cheetos."

We pass peacocks, Mongolian horses and then I see him. Bachuta. Siberian tiger. Four hundred pounds. He is —

— Perfection.

The stupid kid screams and points. And Bachuta turns, barely, calmly, not threatened at all, chill. And Bachuta glances at the kid. And then he looks back. At me.

And we turn in such a way that we are getting even closer about six feet above the barbed wire.

And I'm watching Bachuta and I swear on my children — if I ever have any, on my children's lives — that tiger laughs at me. Not laughs, I'm not even worthy of a laugh. He smirks. Bachuta smirks and turns away like I'm trash.

I step to the edge and hold on to the roof. My left foot's on the seat, right foot on the railing for balance, for power. So I can feel power. Feel like that tiger. And I take off.

The stupid family doesn't even know. I'm in the air and before I even hit the ground, he turns. I see him. I'm in the air, I don't scream or anything but that tiger knows. Bachuta knows.

I land and he's on me. Bam! Teeth into shoulder. I try to move to react. To let him know I'm a man. But I can't. Parts, limbs aren't moving like they should. Bachuta's got me in his mouth and he can tear me apart. He could've chewed on my heart!

But he stops. Because he knew. He knew I was lame. And I'm not talking about the injuries. He knew I would pose no threat.

He drags me a couple of feet and drops me like dirt. But for one second he waits. He stands there. And I reach up. And he lets me touch him.

I pet that tiger. I pet Bachuta.

… Premeditated? Like I was trying to kill myself? No.

Look, everybody in life makes choices. It was not premeditated, not a suicide attempt but a desire to be one with the tiger. Bachuta.

I wanted to be one with the tiger.

Information on this playwright may be found at
https://newplayexchange.org/users/10758/chris-widney

MELANCHOLY ECHO

Robert Alexander Wray

A PASTOR, 40s-60s, having just quit the church, decides to go on a long pilgrimage to map the inner workings of his mind. Midway through his journey he takes stock and ponders aloud.

PASTOR

I have walked and traveled hard, sleeping in parks, barely eating. My cassock's looser now.

It's a hellishly humid night, almost too hot to sleep out. It feels as if the sun's still ablaze.

Odd thoughts strike when you're isolated in your own brain on a long solitary adventure.

Take, for instance, the letter O, that circular letter meaning eternity, perfection. A tragic scream of realization of Greek proportions, a sound of recognition, the shape of choice for so much that is holy, artistic, utilitarian. The most powerful words feature it: God, world, love, gone, soul, home, Oreo.

It's the shape of the world, of the eye. They all have this "O" in common. The fool's O, when he lays it all out to King Lear, saying, "Thou wast a pretty fellow when thou hadst no need to care for her frowning, now thou art an O without a figure … thou art nothing."

I might be losing my mind. Really.

I'm just a weary little pastor. I think I'll just lay here by this tree, and look at that stunning moon, shimmering like it's engulfed in flame.

"Fortune, good night; smile once more, turn thy wheel."

Information on this playwright may be found at
https://newplayexchange.org/users/20961/robert-alexander-wray

ATLAS, THE LONELY GIBBON

Deborah Yarchun

DAVID, 28, a cybercrime journalist, is trying to convince his wife Irene, 28, to let him leave their apartment open to hackers so he can write an article about their household being hacked. As he speaks, Irene is threatening to update their internet router.

DAVID

This is my life too. This is *our* life. They laid off Sarah the other day. And Vick. All of them. We don't know how long until they lay you off. We need me to keep this job, Irene. It's more compelling writing if it's personal. Can you humor me on this one? Please. The fridge exploding is literally the worst thing that could happen. It's the only thing in the space that can be weaponized. Did it kill us? Did it start a fire?

Okay. A small fire. A small fire. Which we contained.

Whoever's janking with our lights, screwing with our sound system — they're harmless. Bored script kiddies. Nothing better to do. What's the worst that could happen? *(Beginning to panic.)* I need this job, Irene. I need it. *We* need it. *(Starting to lose it.)* Oh my God. It's everything. Irene, please. I wanted to be a journalist since I was in the third grade. I don't want to lose it.

I don't want to lose it.

When I was four, my dad lost his job. And it was like the beginning of the end, okay? Listen —

He was down to like five quarters at one point. I'm not shitting you. We're at a market and he's roaming the aisles for like the cheapest thing you can buy to feed us. And I don't understand shit. Really. Nothing. I'm throwing a tantrum in the toy aisle over wanting a stuffed animal.

And you know what he does? He gives up on the food idea. He goes to a claw machine. Puts a quarter in. And he tries to win me a goddamn stuffed animal. And he loses. The first time. Puts another quarter in. Loses a second time. He's literally down to his last quarter. He looks at me, "One more try?" And by this point, I'm staring hungrily at this one stupid stuffed animal.

And his face has this determination, just desperate determination. Like that claw was literally clawing at his last bit of dignity. He puts that last quarter in. And he wins it. And that's love. Right? That's love. But that night, everything's different. Like his shoulders are tenser. The household is tenser. And he starts trying to control everything. We can't have the lights on. He starts trying to control everything in our lives, because he has no control over his own life.

And every night my parents fight, I hold this stuffed turtle like I'm holding onto my life.

I hug this turtle like a life raft. Because at the center of it is love. Right? But it wasn't enough.

We can't lose our jobs. I can't lose my job. I need this job. I can't lose it. We need this job.

Information on this playwright may be found at
https://deborahyarchun.com

GREAT WHITE

Deborah Yarchun

LUIS, 15, is talking to his new friend Brooke, 14, on a beach.
They've bonded over recent traumas in their lives. LUIS' house
recently flooded during a coastal flood. LUIS has convinced Brooke
he's not afraid of anything. He's been trying to help Brooke be less
afraid. Prior to the monologue, Brooke asked LUIS about what it
was like to step into the floodwaters.

LUIS

It's freaky. It's not like the type of flood that comes with rain, the
water just sort of creeps up on you. Water gushes over your legs,
but it's not like standing in the ocean. The ocean's like — *(He*
gestures the gentle motion of the waves.) Swoosh. Swoosh. But flood
water has bits that grab at you. Not living things like jellyfish.
Dead things. Or things that were never alive. And it's not pretty.
Raw sewage floats by. And you don't know what's under the water.

Hey. Close your eyes. You're ankle deep in water at your doorstep.
Stop light's reflected in the water. You can trip in up to six inches
of water. People drive through flooded streets and into a lake and
die. This old man slipped into a canal and drowned. I read about
that. I saw other things. Mostly shit though.

I … I saw something else. Something kind of crazy. Stepped out
of my flooded house … onto our flooded streets. And I went
under. Like underwater in my head. You know? I'd just stepped
out of our flooded living room outside and something in me froze.
And suddenly I was underwater. My eyes were open. And I could
see everything: debris, a kid's bike, all kinds of crap swirling past
my head. And I know it sounds crazy. I heard voices through the
water. Voices from my family, my father. They were all speaking
a language I couldn't understand. But somehow, I understood
what they meant. Reassuring things like, "You'll be okay. You'll

be okay." I felt myself ten years from now watching myself at that very moment — as I stood in the floodwater knowing it was the moment my world changed. And like, I would look back. And always know that moment underwater.

I opened my eyes. I'm mostly dry. Just ankles deep in water, surrounded by shit. I came up. But like the fear stayed under.

Information on this playwright may be found at
https://deborahyarchun.com

RIGHTS & PERMISSIONS